Mysteria

Mysteria
Mysteria, History of the Secret Doctrines & Mystic Rites of Ancient Religions & Medieval and Modern Secret Orders
Author: Otto Henne am Rhyn

Cover image: *Wanderer above the sea of fog,* Caspar David Friedrich
Lay-out: www.burokd.nl

ISBN 978-94-92355-22-5

© 2017 Revised publication by:

VAMzzz Publishing
P.O. Box 3340
1001 AC Amsterdam
The Netherlands
www.vamzzz.com
contactvamzzz@gmail.com

History of the Secret Doctrines &
Mystic Rites of Ancient Religions &
Medieval and Modern Secret Orders

MYSTERIA

Otto Henne am Rhyn

VAMzzz PUBLISHING

Otto Henne am Rhyn
Sankt Gallen, Switzerland, August 26 1828 – Weiz, Styria, Austria-Hungary, May 1 1914

contents

Translator's note

THE MYSTERIES OF the Ancient Grecian religions; the cryptic teachings and occult interpretations of the popular religious beliefs communicated to disciples by the priests in the temples of ancient Egypt, Assyria, and India: the interesting, half fabulous, half historical episode of Pythagoras and the Pythagorean League in Magna Graecia; the mystic, ascetic, and semi-monastic communities of the Therapeutae and the Essenes in Palestine a century before the birth of Jesus Christ; the later developments of Mysticism in the time of the Roman Empire, as seen in the history of Apollonius of Tyana and in Isis worship, Mithras worship, worship of the Great Mother, etc.; the secret creed and rites of the Knights Templar and the usages of the lodges of the Stonemasons in the Middle Age; the constitution and procedure of the Femgerichte of Westphalia in the fourteenth and fifteenth centuries; the origin and history and the aims of Freemasonry, Rosicrucianism, Illuminism, and a swarm of honest and fraudulent secret organizations in modern' times: all these topics

have before been made subject-matter of numerous learned trac-
tates or of popular compends; but hitherto these doctrines, rites,
associations, have not been studied in their unity, in their mutual
relation. One service which the author of this work renders to the
student of this particular phase of human psychology the longing
for mystery and secret associations is that he develops this rela-
tionship, thus enabling the reader to get a clear understanding of
the whole subject.

But the author does very much more than to coordinate the
facts of mystic associations. He is both a scholar and an artist. Having amassed whatever information regarding the Mysteries and
allied phenomena is accessible in universal literature, he handles
his materials with the skill of a consummate master of style and of
the art of popular exposition. The result is a history of the ancient
Mysteries and of their counterparts and imitations in later times,
as authentic as the most painstaking research could make it, yet
possessing all the charm and grace of a literary masterpiece.

Joseph Fitzgerald

PART FIRST
Mysteries of the East and of Barbarous Nations

1. Introduction

IN ALL AGES mystery has had a special attraction for mankind. Curiosity is innate in us. The child asks about everything, What is this, what is it for, why is it made so, or so? The child fairly harries its parents with questions, never wearies of raising new ones, often so unexpected and so difficult, that it would puzzle the wisest philosopher to answer them. And this instinct of inquiry is dominant in the adult, too. The grown man wants to know what is to be found behind every curtain, every locked door, in every sealed letter. And when sated with such trifles he must push inquiry further, into the infinite; must lift the veil that hides the wondrous image at Sais; must pluck from the forbidden tree of knowledge the tempting golden fruit. He would with the Titans storm heaven, and ascend to heights "where stirs no breath of air, where stands the boundary-stone of creation." At last when Faust, after manifold crosses and disappointments, sees that "we can know nothing," the thought "consumes the heart within him."

And so we must ever be worried by the reflection that the great riddle of existence will not be solved; nay, never can be solved.

Why, we ask, why does anything exist at all? and what does exist, whence comes it, and whither does it go? And though oceans of ink were written on worlds of paper to define the relation between the Here and Beyond, we should not know, after it all, the lot of the thought-endowed tenant of the narrowest human brain-case after its term of living is reached. Never shall we be able to comprehend Being as having a beginning and an end, but neither shall we ever understand how, without beginning or end, it may endure forever, and extend limitless ever farther and farther into the shoreless ocean of the All. The thinker must by force refrain himself from such inference, lest his brain should be seized by delirium; and the progressive man of action turns to what is sure and clear and understandable, while the listless disciple of Buddha, despairing of ever comprehending existence, longs for nirvana, the soul's state of everlasting rest and freedom from cares.

Mankind, then, is encompassed by a vast mystery which never has been discovered, though it presses upon us with force all around, and though we know it exists and are conscious that it attends us at every step we take. But man is too proud to endure the thought that anything is beyond his powers: man must in all things do what the primordial creative power does. The Eternal Incomprehensible created worlds that no mortal eye can see: man with the help of glasses sees them. The Eternal set worlds circling around worlds in such wise that for long we mortals were led into error, and took the earth to be the centre of the universe: but men made calculations and measurements, and discovered that their giant sphere was but a grain of sand among colossal worlds. The Eternal caused mountains to rise and rivers to flow, man, too, piled up mountains and scooped out river-beds and seas. Immense oceans separated the continents: man navigated the oceans and discovered shores never seen before. The lightning, issuing from the clouds, rends asunder great trees that have stood for centuries: man imitates the lightning, and employs the electric current for sending messages across continents and oceans, and for illumination. Steam, vapor of water, he harnesses to his car, or employs it to propel ships across the seas. He takes the sun's rays and makes of them a limner's pencil. Even the Eternal himself man fashions after his own thoughts, and gives to him a name and attributes, a throne and a court, a form, and even a son. And lest he should in any point fail of acting like the Unsearchable, man sets over against the grand everlasting mystery of creation and eternity, which he cannot comprehend, other mysteries of his own invention the mystery of the Incarnation, the Resurrection, Redemption, the Trinity, and the rest; and requires his fellow men to acknowledge and reverence these things as mysteries, and to worship as truth what man's own self-conceit has devised in rivalry with the Eternal.

Thus are mysteries of man's invention propagated from generation to generation. The love of mystery is contagious; the one who hears of mysteries will himself invent more, and with them impose upon others. And the Initiates shut themselves up in secret chambers, swear fearful oaths never to betray to anyone what others know already, employ emblems which they interpret in one sense or another, speak in language peculiar to themselves, exchange special signs with one another, whisper to each other mysterious words, admit persons to their secret associations with direful or with harmless tests and rites, and form aristocracies of intellect, of creed, or of benevolence, of art or of science, even of humor and of folly. Such is the origin of mystic teachings and secret societies, the teachings designed to hold the societies together, and the societies to propagate the teachings: one hand washes the other. In all ages, among all races we find these mysteries existing under the most various forms, and for ends the most diverse, but they all have this in common that they shut out the profane (outsiders), and that their end is to win and hold power and influence. But they have also had secondary aims such as could be attained without secret doctrines or secret association; and these aims have been of all kinds. Now the purpose may be to promote social freedom and religious or scientific enlightenment, anon to repress these; again, it may be to enrich the members, or, on the other hand, to stimulate them to self-sacrificing charity; or a society will have for its object the Beautiful, and will create works of art to glorify the Eternal, but another society will despise whatever is ideal, professing contempt for the world and themselves; or the aim may be nothing short of the destruction of all human society and a return to Chaos.

A variegated picture and full of life! At the head of the moving procession stalk priests in long robes, begarlanded, carrying the sacred image of Isis or chanting hymns to the Eleusinian Demeter. Then come the wild-eyed troops of the Bacchantes, and in sharp contrast to these, philosophers of the Pythagorean League, in white cloaks, looking down on the populace with a smile of mild scorn; after these the unpretending Essenes, who shoulder the cross of suffering, the Roman brotherhoods (collegia), and then the English and German gilds of stonemasons, with hammer, compass, and square; the Knights Templar, in white cloaks blazoned with the red cross, their haughty mien betraying contempt of all authority; the Fathers of the Company of Jesus, in black cassock and four-cornered hat, eyes sanctimoniously downcast, every man of them a corpse in the hands of his superiors; then come seigneurs and scholars and men of every condition, in white aprons and blue ribbons, and last of all an indistinguishable multitude of variously-clad figures. Let us contemplate the several groups of this picture. First, the priests of the so-called heathen religions of antiquity. Here we have men using a twofold manner of speech. To the people they gave out a teaching different from that communicated to the Initiates of their secret associations, their mysteries. How came that about, how is it accounted for, and how can it be justified?

2. The Gods

TO ANSWER THESE questions we must study the origin of religious ideas and the forms they assumed in different periods. Here we meet a phase of thought which stands related to the vain attempts to fathom the Eternal, to scrutinize the Unsearchable, and which, therefore, is necessarily connected with the earliest expression of man's love of the mysterious.

In the dim ages before the dawn of civilization, when the cave-dweller, or the lake-dweller, had completed his day's work, and his. children were in safety for the night, and their hunger stilled, then, in the glad Consciousness of duty discharged, he would rise above mere sense, and would contemplate his surroundings with greater attention than would be possible amid his hard labors as bread winner. Then, surely, what most profoundly impressed his imagination was the blue vault of the sky across which by day the sun, source of light and warmth, or of blazing and scorching heat, and at night the mild-faced moon, diffusing her witching beams, and the innumerable twinkling stars glided in strange unalterable series. Beneath the arch lay extended the surrounding country, and the roan gazed on the diversified panorama of snowdecked alp, roaring cataract, mirror-like lake, and verdant daisy-gemmed prairie. Or he contemplated the tossing billows of the sea, the dread phenomena of the thunder clap and the lightning flash, the ravages of the hurricane, the crash of mountains rent by internal forces, the pitiless, headlong sweep of the river that has overflowed the plain.

These manifestations of the forces of nature, whether winsome or fearsome, impressed the man; and acknowledging his nothingness and impotence he prostrated himself before them and worshiped them. But in worshiping the forces of nature, he must needs think of them as a personality; and the process of personification necessarily began with the phenomena which possess the most pronounced individuality, viz., on the earth, rocks, mountains, trees, animals, rivers, lakes; in the sky, the sun, moon, and stars; between earth and sky, the clouds, winds, thunder, and lightning; finally, fire, the production of which was the first step in human culture.

The further observation of nature led man from particular to general concepts: those were formed more easily, these were hard to compass, and to understand their import required a greater power of reflection. Mythology had its origin in the simple worship of nature, and in this wise.

In the mind of the man who knows nothing of the true relations oi the heavenly bodies, all existence must be divided into two principal categories, heaven overhead, earth underfoot. Heaven and Earth that is the beginning of all mythologies and cosmogonies. Heaven and Earth are for the Israelite the first works of the Eternal; for the Chinese they are "father and mother of all things"; for the Hellenes and the Teutons the first divine beings (Uranos and Gaea, Wodan and Ertha). As men further considered the question how this whole scene of nature, both in its grateful and in its terrible aspects, came to be, Heaven and Earth were regarded as sexed beings, Heaven as fructifying, noble, lofty, male, controlling the lightning and thunder; Earth as prolific, conceptive, passive, female. Heaven and Earth formed a union, and Sun, Moon, and Stars were reputed their children. Among the heavenly bodies the first place is held by the Sun, god of day, who, at his rising in the East by magic power compels his brother and sister deities to obey him: he reigns alone in a sea of light and splendor. Sister and consort of the Sun is the Moon, and the course of these! two across the heavens, their rising and their setting, their shining and their obscuration are the source of endless fanciful myths: in these myths, however, there are frequent transformations, the same hero being now the Sun, again Heaven, and the same heroine being now the Moon, anon the Earth. And phantasy discovered in Sun and Moon so many diverse properties that it separated these from one another, and by degrees formed out of them distinct personalities. The Sun, rising out of the ocean and again sinking into it, became Poseidon (Neptune), and the invisible Sun that through the night tarries in the underworld became god of the world of shades, Pluto; and so with other phenomena of the sun. The Moon, too, in her different forms of waxing, full, and waning moon, rising and setting moon, gives rise to groups of three or four sisters (Graces, Fates, Furies), and to many other forms of goddesses, and these are sad, austere, chaste, or alluring, winsome, complaisant; or the Moon assumes the form of some fair daughter of man, who, being loved by some god, becomes mother of gods and heroes. Hence god-descended races and dynasties, whose fortunes and wars are the subject of epics, tragedies, and romances, and the innumerable host of the stars, in the fanciful shapes in which imagination grouped them, afforded inexhaustible material for story and myth. Here was seen a herd faithfully guarded by the herdsman, there a chase conducted by bold hunters, or a company of daring mariners going to win the golden fleece, or the golden apples of the Hesperides, or the thousand eyes of the watchful Argus. On the mantle of the goddess of night phantasy saw pictured Aries, Taurus, Capricornus, Capella, Ursus Major, Orion, Bootes, Draco, Hercules, and all the other figures of the endless web of poesy in which are told the wondrous deeds of gods and heroes.

Such is the light in which mythology appeared when, in the beginnings of scientific inquiry, the forces of nature were personified. As centuries passed the true sense of these myths, transmitted from father to son, was lost, and the whole was taken to be actual fact. But the master minds discerned the true state of the case, and soon regained the real meanings. Such men as Aristotle, Plutarch, and others often told in their writings what they thought regarding the traditions, but not so the wily priests within the walls of the temples. Their secret doctrines doubtless conveyed a more or less rationalistic interpretation of the myths and a purer theology, though it must be admitted that, in order to guard the mysteries of the secret associations, and to save the priesthood from becoming superfluous, this teaching was tricked out in mysticism, symbolism and allegory; and above all that it was accompanied by certain dramatic representations and certain moralizing, ceremonies.

The countries of antiquity whereof we know with certainty that they possessed "mysteries," i. e., secret associations under priestly guidance, are Egypt, Chaldaea, and Greece.

3. Egypt

AS THE SOURCES of the Nile were undiscovered till a very recent date, so do the sources of Egyptian civilization remain hidden still. We know fairly well how the population of Egypt was made up. It consisted of an aboriginal stock, whose physical characters, as given in writings or in sculptures, show that it was of negro origin, and of a conquering people belonging to the same race as the inhabitants of Europe in high antiquity: this race invaded the Nile land probably from Asia, made themselves masters of it, and 'in time mingled with the aborigines. The great moving cause of Egyptian civilization was always the Nile, called in Egypt Hapi; for the Nile was the essential factor, by the annual overflow of its fertilizing waters in Summer and Autumn, in determining the conformation of the land, the climate, the seasons, and, consequently, the manners and usages of the inhabitants. Hence in the language of the natives, Egypt was called Kemt, the dark land, because of the rich deposits of loam left after the floods of the Nile.

But this name attached only to the Nile valley, bounded on the East and West by stony deserts, which the Egyptians did not reckon as belonging to their country. The Semites called the land Misr, or Misraim; the Greeks gave first to the river, then to the region, the name Egypt (on what grounds we know not), and finally to the river the name Neilos. It has ever been a land of enigmas, this Nileland. Whence comes its river? Why does it overflow the country in Summer and Autumn? Why those mighty pyramids? What were the doings in those temples, planted so close together? What mean those strange characters, the hieroglyphs? Why do the gods wear heads of animals, and why, on the other hand, have the sphinxes a human head on a lion's body?

In order to exercise undisputed mastery over the country the conquerors divided among themselves all the land and all the authority. They formed two' hereditary classes or estates Priests, who controlled the minds, and Warriors, who controlled the bodies of the conquered people. Of the subject race there were several classes, most probably six, though the accounts we have are mutually contradictory. These classes are: Artists, mechanics, traders, mariners, agriculturists, herdsmen; in the latter class of the swineherds, most despised of all Egyptians, because of the unclean animal which they tended.

Now, while the warrior class had the management of military affairs and the executive government, and as a rule supplied the occupants of the throne, the priests possessed the legal lore and the scientific knowledge, and prescribed to the people what they must believe, while among themselves and in the company of Initiates they thought very differently.

The Egyptian religion has its foundation in astronomy. The regular overflow of the Nile, which involved a precise division of the year into seasons, must at an early period have led to a diligent observation of the course of the stars, in order to make timely preparation for the floods; and the splendor of the starry sky in that region, near the tropics, where hardly a single constellation is out of sight through the whole year, favored the study of astronomic science.' The Egyptians contemplated the glories of the heavens, not with the stolidity of the Chinese, who therein see only objects to be counted and measured; nor yet with the idealist imagination of Europeans. Hence their personifications of the world of stars are uncouth, confused, without grace or charm.

The heavenly body that for us is mightiest of all, the sun, must have been for the Egyptians the most ancient and the mightiest of gods. Their sun-god was named Re. But even as among the Hellenes, so in Egypt the several attributes of the sun were assigned to different personalities. Thus, the rising sun, as the youthful warrior-god Horos, was early distinguished from Re; over against Horos stood his opposite and his twinbrother, Set, spirit of darkness. For mothers the sungod had Isis, Hathor, and Neit, goddesses of heaven. To these deities were added Aah, the moon-god, and the gods of the several stars and constellations. Besides these gods of the whole land, particular places and regions had their own gods; thus Ptah was lord and god of Memphis, Amon of Thebes, and so on.

Very often certain worshipful objects, as trees and animals inhabited by spirits, were developed into local deities. In this way the tetichism of the black aboriginal people got entry into the more cultured religion of the light-complexioned conquerors, and had a very powerful influence on it. Few were the indigenous animals that were not worshiped in one place or in many as the wrappages of deities. That worship was paid to animals not for their own sake, is best seen from the way in which the gods are portrayed, namely, for the most part with a human body and the head of the animal sacred to them, though in some cases entirely in human form. Thus Amon, god of Thebes, has the head of a ram, Hathor of Anut the head of a cow, Anubis that of a jackal, Bast that of a cat, Sechet of a lioness, Sebak of a crocodile, and so on. And inasmuch as it was believed that gods dwelt in them, such animals were themselves made objects of worship; for example, the ox Hapi (Gr. Apis) at Memphis, the goat at Mendes, and so forth. This honor belonged to the entire species, and as representing the species, certain individual animals were maintained in the temples by the contributions of the faithful, and had servitors to wait upon them. Any harm done to these fetiches was sternly punished: to kill one of them was death. Not so when a god did not grant the prayers of the faithful, e.g., for rain: in that case the priests made the fetich pay the penalty. First, they threatened the animal, but when menaces were vain, they killed the sacred beast, though in secret; the people must not know of it.

4. The Higher Development of Egyptian Religion

AS EGYPT ADVANCED in civilization and the government became more concentrated, the local deities and idolatry were less regarded, while the light-gods, the sungods, Re and Kcros, with their associate deities, became most prominent. The lives and fortunes of these light gods, and in particular their wars with the powers of darkness, became the subject of myths. The inhabitants of the Nile valley imagined to themselves the sun's course not as the progress of a chariot like that in which the Mithra of the Persians and the Helios of the Greeks were borne, but as the voyage of a Nile bark on which Re navigates the ocean of the heavens. In the battle with dark Set he falls and drops into the netherworld in the West, but the youthful Horos, sun-god of the coming day, takes his place and begins his career across the sky. This ever-rejuvenescent sun-god, who through all transformations remained still the same deity, so that the selfsame goddess was now his mother, anon his consort, was so truly the supreme god, nay, the sole god of Egypt, that his hieroglyph, the sparrowhawk, came to be the. sign of the idea "god," and in writing that sign was attached to the names of gods to indicate that they were such. On the other hand, the names of the mothers and consorts of the sun-gods had appended to them the sign for a cow.

From this it "is seen that the religion of Nileland that is to say, the religion of the priests was slowly progressing toward monotheism. Unlike the beliefs of the commonalty, the secret teachings or mysteries of the priests, as gradually developed, regarded not simply the existence of the gods, but, above all, what the gods stood for. For a while this development halted at the sun-god, and reached its first stage in the city Anu (in lower Egypt), called by the Greeks Heliopolis (city of the sun), where they incorporated the god of the place, Turn, in the sungod Re. This took place under the fourth dynasty, whose monarchs built the great pyramids of Ghizeh at Memphis. But one of the greatest of these transformations was in giving the name of Osiris, god of the city Abdti (Gr. Abydos) in upper Egypt, to the god of the sunset, ruler of the netherworld and of the kingdom of death. Isis became his sister and consort, Set at once his brother and his slayer, Horos his son, who, as a new sun, takes his place after sunset, and also his avenger on Set. Horos gives Set battle, but as he cannot destroy him utterly, leaves to him the desert as a kingdom, while Horos himself holds the Nile valley. This story of gods was represented scenically on public holidays, but only the Initiated, i. e., the priests and their followers who had been let into the secret, knew the meaning of the representation. Even the name of Osiris and his abode in the realm of the dead were kept secret, and outsiders heard only of the "great god" dwelling in "the West." Besides the mysteries of Osiris, the most famous of all, there were other mysteries of local Egyptian gods transformed into sun-gods; and so the sun mythos was further developed. Thus Thot, god of Hermopolis, whose sacred animal was the bird Ibis, became Horos's auxiliary in the war with Set, and also became the moon-god, the god of chronometry and of order, inventor of writing, revealer of the sacred books. Memphis alone, capital of the ancient kingdom, held her god Ptah too exalted a being to share in the transformation of the rest; for Ptah was regarded by his worshipers as father of all gods, creator of the world and of men, and more ancient than Re; besides, he was the god of the royal court. Nevertheless, he did not escape the fate of becoming a sun-god. The most celebrated object of Egyptian zoolatry was sacred to Ptah, namely, Apis (Hapi), the sacred bull of Memphis, symbol of the sun and also of the fructifying "Nile. This bull must be black with a white spot on the forehead, and with a growth under the tongue having the form of the sacred beetle. The bull was kept in the temple at Memphis from calfhood till death; the body was then mummified, laid out in state, and honored with inscriptions as a god. The behavior of Apis in various conjunctures and circumstances was reputed to be oracular.

Another form of the sun-god was the Sphinx, a halfhuman, half-brute figure in stone, repeated a thousand times in the Nile valley. The most famous sphinx of all is seen at the great pyramids of Ghizeh. Regular avenues flanked by sphinxes formed the approaches of the great temples. In Egypt the sphinx was thought of as male; the head was that of some king, and the whole figure represented the sun-god Harmachis, a name compounded of Re and Horos (Ra-Harm-chuti). In later times the sphinx was introduced in Asia and Greece; the Grecian sphinx is always female.

When the local deities of Egypt were reduced to system, Re was still supreme, but now Re had a father, Nunu, god of Chaos, source of all being clearly a product of priestly meditation, quite alien to the popular mind. Re was the first divine ruler of the earth. The stars were his companions. He was succeeded by his son Shu (represented with a lion's head), god of air, who made the props that sustain the sky. Shu was followed by the god Keb and the goddess Nut, parents of Osiris and Isis, who then became the earth's rulers. To them, after Set's usurpation, succeeded Horos the avenger and the goddess Hathor. A second class comprises the inferior gods, as Thot, Anubis, etc.; and in a third class are the local deities. The number of gods and of daemons subordinate to them was enormous. But in their gods the Egyptians looked not at all for the perfection of goodness, nor did they regard right behavior as essential for gaining heavenly favor; they rather looked on the practices of religion frankly as a means of advancing their individual interests with the gods.

Now, the greater the number of gods the less was the difference between ithem, and the easier became the transition to the belief in the sun-god as supreme and only true deity a belief entertained by the priesthood, not by the people. Re became for the priests the one god, creator of the universe; and this was due to the fact that the priests of the foremost cities, following the example of those of Heliopolis, praised the local god as supreme over all, and at the same time made him identical with Re, whose name was appended to the original name, thus, Turn-Re, Amon-Re. When Thebes became the capital of the kingdom its god Amon naturally took the foremost place, and while Thebes flourished, in the beginning of the so-called new empire, it was known to all Initiates that the sun-god was the one true god, self-created, sole object of the worship paid to the innumerable host of other gods. Nay, the evil deity Set came to pass for a form of Re, and was allowed a place in the Sun's bark. Self-creation was also attributed to the moon-god. The king, as lord of the whole country, prayed in identical words in every place to the local deity as lord of heaven and earth.

5. A Reformation in the Land of Nile

BUT NOW THE secret doctrine of the priests was to be published to the people. The pharao Amenhotep IV., of the 18th dynasty (about 1460 B.C.), saw in the power of the priesthood a menace to the dignity of the crown. He therefore proclaimed as the sole god the sun, not under any human form, as had been the custom, but in its own proper shape of a disk (in Egyptian, aten), as had been the usage at Heliopolis. Amenhotep ordered all images of other gods associated with the sun to be destroyed, assumed for himself the name Chuenaten, "Splendor of the Sundisk," quit Thebes, and built in middle Egypt, east of the Nile, a new royal seat, Chutaten, "abode of the Sundisk." The priests of the deposed gods in Thebes and in certain other cities (not in all) lost their places, and the great estates of the priestly corporations were confiscated. Of course the court officers and civil functionaries loyally followed the example of their master; but only a very small fraction of the priesthood gave up their convictions for the sake of livelihood.

Hardly was Chuenaten gathered to his fathers after a reign

of twelve years, when his reform was undone. His sons-in-law, who succeeded him, returned step by step to the religion of Amon, and again fixed the royal seat at Thebes; nevertheless, they were held to be heretics by the priests, now reinstated in their ancient power. The temples erected to the Sundisk were leveled with the ground, the half-completed city of the sun was obliterated, the confiscation of the estates of priestly corporations reversed, and the temples, images, and priesthood of Amon reinstated. The intellectual life of Egypt was thenceforth paralyzed, and the ancient mystic teachings of the priests were never again disturbed by any wave of movement or progress. The people went back to stupid formalism, and sank even deeper into dae-monism and sorcery. To draw them away from the true god the priests taught them to worship deceased kings and queens, at the same time amusing them with gorgeous sacrifices processions, and festivals. The distance separating the priesthood from the people and the Pharaos were, though not of the priestly class, reckoned as compeers of the priests was signalized by the temples with their various compartments in the inmost of which, the holy of holies (adyton), were guarded the mysteries of the priests, while the people were admitted only to the temple proper and its forecourt. In all probability the famed Labyrinth near Lake Moeris, at Crocodilopolis, was designed for priestly ends. The labyrinth was an underground maze of chambers. Herodotus tells that there were 1,500 chambers above ground and as many under the surface, and that the underground chambers were not shown to the profane, for they contained the remains of Pharaos and ot sacred crocodiles. Not Herodotus only, but Diodorus, Strabo, and Pliny cel-ebrate the glory of this vast palace, in whose hidden compartments, no doubt, fit quarters were found for the mysteries.

6. The Egyptian Realm of the Dead

FINALLY, THE SECRET teaching of the priests played a part in the people's ideas regarding death and the other life. According to the Egyptian teaching, man is made up of three constituent parts, viz., besides the body, the soul (ba), conceived to be of purely material essence, which at death quitted the body in the form of a bird; and the immaterial spirit (ka), which held to the man the same relation a god held to the animal in which he dwelt: at death the spirit departed from the body like the image of a dream. The gods, too, had their ka and their ba. The continued existence of both soul and spirit was contingent on the care the corpse received; if the ka and the ba were to live on, the body must be embalmed and laid in a chamber hollowed in a rock, or in a sepulchral edifice (of such buildings the pyramids were the most notable), and the relatives must supply to the dead meat and drink and clothing. The spirit of the deceased went to Osiris, lord of the other world a luxuriant plain (Aaru) in the West, where the earth's products required no toil, but grew spontaneous. By means of the magic formula with which Horos recalled to life the slain Osiris, the dead is riot only in like manner revivified, but is even made one with Osiris; and hence in the formulas of funeral service which constitute the so-called "Book of the Dead," the deceased is addressed as Osiris with addition of his own name. Therefore, he may now sail in the sun-bark, and lead a glorious life in the other world, and walk amid the stars like other gods. The pictures on the walls of the sepulchral chambers show that the Egyptians conceived the other life to be much like the present, only pleasanter and fuller. The deceased is portrayed surrounded by such enjoyments as were attainable in Nileland banquets, property, the chase, voyaging, music, and the like. But from the texts of the "Book of the Dead," which used to be laid with the dead in the sepulchre, we see that these representations had a more spiritual import in the "middle" than in the "old" empire. In these texts the deceased himself speaks, identifying himself with some god, or with one god after another; no longer with Osiris only, for according to the developed teaching of that time all the gods are one god. The route of the dead toward the other world is the sun's track from East to West; but on his journey he needs the help of the sorcerer's art against the host of daemons and monsters that threaten him. Arrived there, he acquires the power of revisiting the earth at will in the form of god, man, or animal, or even, should he so choose, in his own former body. At this period puppets made of wood or of clay, and sundry tools and utensils, were laid in the grave with the dead for their service. Under the "new empire" the representations of the other life and of the way thither are more detailed and more fanciful. Here, too, we find representations of the famous "judgment of the dead," an event belonging to the life beyond, and not, as the Greeks mistakenly supposed, to the present state and to the time immediately before burial. Osiris presides over the tribunal with two-and-forty assessors, in whose presence the newcomer has to prove himself guiltless of any one of two-and-forty sins, thus, for example: "Never have I done an injustice, never have I stolen, never have I craftily compassed the death of any man, never have I killed any sacred animal," etc. Yet all this was rather a magic formula for attaining blessedness according to Egyptian notions than a truthful protestation of guiltlessness in order to establish the postulant's moral purity. Nevertheless, in a picture of the Judgment of the Dead in the "Book of the Dead" the deceased is brought by the goddess of truth and righteousness (Ma) into the palace of Osiris, and his sins and his good deeds are weighed in a balance. The hippopotamus is present as accuser and the god Thot as defender.

7. The Secret Teaching of the Priests of Nileland

THOUGH FROM THE foregoing we get a general notion of the relation between the priests and the people, still we are not clear as to the nature of the secret teaching and the mode of its organization. Here we have to depend almost entirely on the accounts given by Greek writers, not always trustworthy, and on conjecture or inference.

Unquestionably the secret doctrine necessitated a species of secret society which presumably consisted of the higher orders of priests, and which comprised subdivisions only loosely held together. It is stated positively that the pharao for the time being was always admitted to membership. Hence the king was the only

Egyptian outside of the priestly order that was acquainted with the secret doctrine, and thus was all danger of betrayal at home most effectually averted. But as the priests had less to fear in this regard from foreigners, because foreigners went away again; and as in the indoctrination of foreigners the priests saw an opportunity for cultivating their own reputation for erudition, therefore they often willingly admitted to initiation men of distinction from abroad, and especially Greeks. Among the fabulous personages who were believed to have been impelled by thirst for knowledge to visit Egypt, there to learn the secret wisdom of the priests, were the bards Orpheus, Musaeus, and Homer; among the historic characters were the lawgivers Lycurgus and Solon, the historian Herodotus, the philosophers Thales, Pythagoras, Plato, Democritus, the mathematician Archimedes, and very many more. But it was not always easy for these to lift the veil that hid the mysteries. Pythagoras, for example, though recommended by King Aahmes (Amasis), applied in vain to the priests of Heliopolis and Memphis, and only after he had submitted to the circumcision prescribed for postulants did he receive from the priests of Diospolis instruction in their recondite sciences.

In the form of admission to this secret doctrine were long and tedious but significant ceremonies, and the Initiates had at certain intervals to ascend a number of degrees, or stages of knowledge, till they mastered the sum of the wisdom taught by the priests. But with regard to the mode of this progression and the difference between the degrees we have unfortunately no reliable testimony.

Of the contents of the Egyptian secret teaching we know little more than we do of its forms, for all Initiates were pledged to strictest silence regarding the subject matter of instruction. Yet we are not without scattered hints from competent authorities, and in the light of these we cannot go seriously astray. According to the Greek historian Diodorus, who lived in the time of Julius Caesar and Augustus, and who had himself been initiated in Egypt, Orpheus, or rather the Orphic mystae named after him, owed the Grecian mysteries to the priests of Egypt; and to the same source were Lycurgus and Solon beholden for their legislation, Pythagoras and Plato for their philosophical systems, and Pythagoras furthermore for his mathematical knowledge, and Democritus for his astronomical doctrine. Now, as for the exact sciences here mentioned, the Egyptian secret teaching could not have comprised anything thereanent which was not attainable by anybody with the scientific helps of the time; nor anything in the way of astronomic knowledge not relating to the calculation of time; and if with regard to this knowledge nothing fundamental was taught to the people, then that was a base huckstering of mysteries and not a secret teaching. As for legislation, the systems of Lycurgus and Solon differ so much from each other, and are so pronouncedly Spartan and Athenian, respectively, in spirit, that from them we cannot infer what the teaching was in that department. The probability is that the two Grecian lawgivers merely used the Egyptian laws as a basis, and for the rest adapted their ideas to the needs of their respective countries. Nor is it to be assumed that because the Egyptian priests were also judges, therefore their ideas on legislation, which assuredly they must have applied freely and above board, belonged to their mysteries.

From the hieroglyphic remains, however, it appears that there existed in Egypt high-grade schools conducted by the priests, and hence we may infer that in these institutions the Greek searchers after knowledge obtained instruction in lawgiving and in the exact sciences of the Egyptians.

It is true that the hieroglyphs, a species of Egyptian writing which consisted of figures of actual objects, were known only to the priests; but in early times that was so only because the rest of the people could not read and write. Afterward there was a special popular form of writing (demotic) derived from the hieroglyphs and resembling an earlier abbreviated form of hieroglyphic writing, the hieratic or writing of the priests.

It is different with philosophical and religious speculation, in which positive, unimpeachable conclusions such as may be had in the exact sciences, are out of the question, and which has no practical application as in jurisprudence and diplomatics; which, in feet, gives play rather to hypothesis and arbitrary opinion, to mysticism and symbolism. This, therefore, was the subject matter of the teaching conveyed to Initiates in the Egyptian mysteries, but for good reasons then withheld from the vulgar, because here the very existence of the priestly class was at stake: the priesthood would lose all its importance once the people were aware that the priests had no regard for the received religion.

Hence there is no doubt that the secret doctrine of the Egyptian priests was at once philosophic and religious; that is, that it tested the traditional belief, analyzed it, and accepted what it found to be reasonable and rejected what appeared irrational; and it was sharply distinguished from the popular belief, which took tradition for absolute and indubitable truth.

What, then, were the principles underlying the philosophic religion of the Egyptian priests? Putting aside all arbitrary and fine-drawn theories, we infer from various clear indications that it was of a monotheistic character, i. e., that it postulated one personal god, and that it rejected polytheism and zoolatry, as well as the materialistic conceptions of the popular creed with regard to what takes place after death. Indeed, we hold it not improbable that the secret doctrine was often more radical than the views of the royal reformer Amenhotep IV., or Chuenaten, and that, unlike him, the priests believed the true god to be, not a material thing, the sun's disk, but the unseen creator himself, called by them Nunu, father of Re, and source of all things. Thus we find in the "Book of the Dead" and in later writings mention of a "demiurge (or architect) of the universe," to whom no special divine name is given. Plutarch, too, in his ingenious work, "Of Isis and Osiris" (cc. 67, 68), says: "The godhead is not any mindless or soulless creature subject to man," an allusion to zoolatry; and again: "There is only one rational being that orders all things, but one ruling providence, and subordinate powers which are set over the several things and which in different nations receive through traditional usage, distinctive worship and distinctive appellations. And hence Initiates employ now symbols obscure, anon more obvious, whereby they guide the understanding to the divine being, yet not without danger of falling into the mire of superstition or the abyss of unbelief. Therefore must one take philosophy for his mystagogue (guide to the mysteries), in order to have a true understanding of all the teachings and all the rites of the mysteries."

The belief in one personal creator having been accepted, the Egyptian mythology was naturally declared erroneous, and its true signification was expounded by the priests to the initiated. That this interpretation of the myths as allegorical accounts of personified natural phenomena was the essential part of the mysteries appears from the testimonies of learned Greeks, some of them Initiates, e. g., Plutarch ("Isis and Osiris," c. 3) writes: "Not the white vesture and the shaven beard make the servant of Isis: he alone is truly that, who receives due instruction upon the rites and ceremonies used in that divine service, who investigates judiciously, and meditates upon the truth therein contained." Again (c. 8): "There is in the rites of the Egyptian priests nothing irrational, nothing fabulous or superstitious. Instead of irrationality we find principles and precepts of morality; instead of fable and superstition, authentic history and facts of nature." And c. 9: "The image of the goddess Neit at Sais, regarded also as the image of Isis, bears this inscription: 'I am the All that was, that is, that is to be; my veil no mortal has ever raised.' Finally, c. 11: "When we hear the Egyptian myths of the gods, their wandering about, their dismemberment and sundry other like incidents, we must recall the remarks already made, so as to understand that the stories told are not to be taken literally as recounting actual occurrences." The more cautious Herodotus (II., 61) agrees with Plutarch, though he expresses himself more enigmatically: "On the festival of Isis in the city of Bubastis, after the sacrifice all, both men and women, thousands of them, beat themselves. But for me to name the one for whose sake they beat themselves were impiety."

All the traditions and rites of the Egyptian popular religion then were explained in a rationalist sense to the initiated. Many particulars of this explanation have been lost, but what has been lost can hardly have been of any real value for us, and is little to be regretted.

8. Babylon and Ninive

IN THE TRADITIONS of classic antiquity the secret wisdom of the Egyptian priests was not held in greater esteem than that of their fellow-priests in Chaldaea or Babylonia, the enlightened empire on the lower Tigris and Euphrates, of which Assyria, land of the upper Tigris, was only a colony. Recent research has brought up the question which civilization was the earlier, that of the Nileland or that of Western Asia, in the region of the twin rivers. But as we possess with regard to the Babylonian religion even less information than with regard to the Egyptian, we must be content with a brief account of it.

The Chaldaean religion beyond a doubt had its origin in the country around the lower Tigris and Euphrates among a people of Turanian or Ural-Altaic stock (akin to the Turks), called Sumerians, or Akkadians: its root was Shamanism, a form of religion peculiar to the Turkic races. The most ancient religious writings of this people (among whom cuneiform writing originated) consist in formulas for exorcising evil spirits; these spirits are usually represented as coming from the desert in groups of seven. Over these daemons presided the spirit of the heavens (In-lilla, afterward called Anu, i. e., sky); after Anu greatest reverence was paid to the spirit of the earth (In-kia or Ea), who was afterward spirit of the waters also. From the higher spirits were evolved gods and goddesses innumerable. The most ancient goddess was Ba-u, a name signifying "primordial water," or chaos. After Ba-u came the "daughter of the heavens," named at first Anun, later Ninni or Ninna, and afterward Istar.

The Sumerian groundwork of Chaldaean civilization and religion was built upon bv a Semitic people, the Babylonians and Assyrians proper, traces of whom are found nearly 4000 years B.C. and whose domination seems established B.C. 2500. The highest god of this race was called simply "God" (in their language Ilu), or "Lord" (Baal). Sun and moon were worshiped as his images. The scene of the life after death was laid in the realm of shades (shualu, in Hebrew Sheol). This religion was blended with that of the Sumerians. The gods Anu and Ilu became one god of the sky, Bel; and Istar became Bel's wife. Other Sumerian gods were associated with the planets worshiped by the Semites: Marduk with Jupiter, Ninclar with Saturn, Nirgal with Mars, Nabu with Mercury, while Istar was specially related to Venus. There was a sort of trinity made up of Samas (sun), Sin (moon), Ramnian (god of storms). Similarly, Anu, spirit of the sky, and Ea, spirit of the earth, were placed side by side with Bel. This system was completed about 1,900 B.C, and it remained unchanged in Assyria, save that there the autochthonous god Assur held the first place among the gods.

Among the Babylonians and Assyrians the priests were held in great reverence. In Assyria they stood next after the king, and the king was high priest; in the Babylonian kingdom they occupied a more independent and more influential station. Like the priests of Egypt, they probably had a secret doctrine withheld from the vulgar. From the meanings of the Babylonian deities' names, as given above, it is easy to infer the nature of this secret doctrine. The Chaldees were throughout all antiquity known as observers of the heavenly bodies. And though probably they were astrologers rather than astronomers, at least they knew enough about the stars, the heavens, and the facts of meteorology to regard them for what they were instead of holding them to be gods. We therefore believe that the Chaldaean priests among themselves looked on the objects which before the people they held to be gods as simply sky, sun, moon, planets, lightning, thunder.

Besides the early cuneiform writings already mentioned (forms of exorcism), there have been found amid the ruins of Babylon great "libraries" of writings on tiles, in the cuneiform characters. Among these are "penitential psalms" and hymns to gods. In the following psalm, deciphered from the tile tablets, a priest, in the name of a penitent sinner, entreats the goddess.

O Lady, for thy servant the cup is full.
Speak the word to him, "Let thy heart be tranquil."
Thy servant-evil have I done
Give him assurance of mercy.
Turn thy countenance himward.
Consider his entreaty.
Thy servant, thou art angry with him.

Be to him gracious.
Lady, my hands are tied.
I cling to thee.

Many of the mythological poems, indeed, most of them, and great part of the less sacred literature of the tablets, are so obscure and unintelligible that for their understanding a "key" was necessary, and the priests held the key. Of special interest are the fragments containing portions of the Babylonian cosmogony; and as our Bible (Gen. xi., 31) tells that Abraham was of Ur in Chaldaea, his descendants would inherit from him (supposing him to have been an historical personage) some portions of the ancient traditions and folklore of the Chaldaeans. Here is a fragment of the Babylonian story of the Creation:

When the sky above was not yet named.
Earth beneath had yet no name,
and the watery deep, the never-beginning,
was their producer.
the chaos of the sea, genderess of them all,
for her waters united together in one.
The darkness was not yet done away,
not a plant had yet budded.
As of the gods none had yet gone forth,
and they yet had no name,
then the great gods, too, were created, etc.

The Chaldee Noah, called Samas-Napishtim (sun of life), tells the story of the deluge in this form: The god Ea having made known to him the punishment decreed for mankind on account of their sins, he built a great ship at the god's command, and into it brought all his possessions, his kinsmen, his servants, also domestic and wild animals. Then the gods let a great tempest loose, and with the spirits entered the combat to destroy all living things. But the flood rose up to the sky and threatened even the lower gods, who had to take refuge with the higher gods. The gods, therefore, repented of what they had done. But after seven days the storm was quieted, and the waters were abated; Samas-Napishtim opened the window of his ship, now resting on the mountain Nizir, and after other seven days freed a dove, but the dove found no resting place. Then a swallow, which did in like manner; then a raven, which preyed on the bodies of the drowned. It was now possible for Samas-Napishtim to let the animals out; he erected an altar and offered sacrifice, whereto the gods gathered "like masses of flies." Then the god Bel, who had ordered the flood, became reconciled with the other gods, who were angry with him on that account; he led Samas-Napishtim forth with his wife, and made a covenant with them and the people. But the pair were taken afar to live for evermore.

This Chaldaic history of the deluge is but one section of a great poem, an epos contained in twelve earthen tablets, wherein are recounted the fortunes and exploits of a hero, apparently the Nimrod of the Hebrew Bible. This poem is reputed to date from the twenty-third century, B.C. The deeds of this hero, Gishdubarra, or Namrassit, as he is called, forcibly recall the story of the Hellenic Herakles, and the Heraclean myth, perhaps, had its origin in the Chaldaean epos. Gishdubarra is a descendant of Samas-Napishtim, whom he seeks out in his retreat to obtain a cure of his disease, and who takes that occasion to narrate to him the history of the flood. Now, his disease was a visitation of the goddess Anatu, because that he had spurned the love of the goddess Istar. A short poem graphically and effectively tells of how Istar in her distress over this repulse sought help in the netherworld. "Istar's Descent into Hell" impresses one like Dante's "Inferno"; indeed, in the opening verses it employs nearly the same words as the great Florentine. Istar goes, says the poet,

> *To that 'house whence none comes forth that enters,*
> *On that path that allows advance, but regress never;*
> *To that house whose inmates light shall see nevermore,*
> *To that place where dust is 'their victual and ordure their*
> *meat, etc.*

In the netherworld the goddess Allatu reigns as queen. She is Istar's counterpart: as Istar (daughter of the moon-god) is the rising moon, or the morning-star, so is Allatu the setting moon, or the evening-star. The two are the mutually conflicting opposite sides of one being; and here, perhaps, we have an intimation of a deeper ethical interpretation, according to the secret doctrine of the Chaldaeans. The hell of the Chaldaean theology is divided into seven compartments separated by gates. At each gate Istar must surrender to its keeper some portion of her paraphernalia; at the first the crown, at the second the earrings, at the third the necklace, at the fourth the mantle, at the fifth the girdle, crusted with precious stones, at the sixth the armlets and anklets, and at the seventh the last vesture. Possibly, we have here a symbolic allusion to the Chaldaean mystic teaching, which may have had seven degrees of initiation into as many orders of mysteries, till all were disclosed. The queen of the nether world not only renders to Istar no assistance, but, contrariwise, treats her as an enemy, and heaps bodily injuries upon her. Meanwhile on earth, Istar being the goddess of love, all union of the sexes, whether among men or animals, ceases, and at last the gods request of Allatu the liberation of Istar. Reluctantly she consents. Istar is made whole and set free, and at each gate gets back again what had been taken from her. The poem was intended to be recited by the priest at the obsequies of the dead, to give assurance to the mourning survivors that the gates of the netherworld are not unconquerable, but that there is still a possibility for the shades to reach the land of the blest, the abode of Istar.

9. Zoroaster and the Persians

IF IN CHALDAEA the traces of actual secret teaching seem faint and indistinct, they quite disappear the further we go from the centers of ancient culture in Northern Africa and Western Asia, though analogies are found everywhere. In Persia, whose culture for the rest was an offshoot of that of Chaldaea, the priests (athravan) of

Zarathustra's, or Zoroaster's, religion were the highest of the three classes of the population, and the priestly class was considered further removed from the other two (warriors and farmers) than they from each other. Sprung originally from a Median stock, the priests married only women of their own race, and alone of the population possessed high culture. As in Egypt, the King was adopted into the priestly class. The priests went about the country as teachers, but gave religious instruction only to those of their class. The chief priest was styled Zarathustrotema, i. e., the one nearest to Zarathustra, and had his see in the holy city Ragha (now Rai), whose inhabitants, like those of modern Rome, had the name of being unbelievers. The priests alone held rule in Ragha, and no secular power had right to give orders. Even elsewhere throughout the kingdom the priests regarded themselves as subject only to the commands of the Zarathustrotema. Further, they were physicians, astrologers, interpreters of dreams, scribes, judges, officers of state, etc. The duties they sought to impress upon the minds of the people were these exclusively: That they should reverence the holy fire, listen to the reading of passages from the sacred books, and perform no end of ceremonies of purification on account of their sins against the precepts of their religion. All this points to the existence of a mystic gild of the priests, which withheld the real teachings of their religion from the uninitiated, and the members of which alone understood what was the original of the strife between the good world of Ormuzd and the evil of Ahriman, namely, in all probability, the alternation of night and day, Summer and Winter.

10. Brahmans and Buddhists

THE CASE WAS much the same in India. There the priests, then as now, the highest caste (Brahmans), were separated from the people by even a deeper gulf than in Persia. They can have no communication with people of any other caste, and can take nothing from any one not belonging to their own caste. They stand outside of the state and its laws, and have laws of their own. By the people they are regarded as gods: they and their pupils, the Bramatsharin, as is said in the "Atharva-Beda" (book of ceremonial laws), give life to both worlds; nay, they it is that made sky and earth fast on their foundations, that introduced religion, the gods, and immortality, that produced the world, that brought the daemons into subjection. Thus they indoctrinated the people; but as they themselves of course knew that things were not so, a secret doctrine naturally sprung up among them, and so they instituted a mystic society, whose members alone knew how the matter really stood, and that the people were hoodwinked. Accordingly, the basis of religion was totally different for the Brahmans from what it was for the rest of the people. The latter were idolaters, the former pantheists. This pantheism is taught in all their sacred books; but these books the second and third castes (warriors and farmers) did not understand, and the fourth caste, the servile (which was also the most numerous), durst not read them at all.

According to this doctrine, all gods and the whole creation are sprung from Eternity (Aditi). Penitents and solitaries were esteemed by the Brahmans above kings and heroes, even above gods. But the life of a hermit was not perfect enough for them, for that was attained by the next two castes. Therefore, as their own peculiar specialty, they concocted the idea of a sort of a soul of the universe, the Atman-Brahman (the All-Me, or Me-All). This dogma was originated by the Brahman Yadshnavalkva: but Brahmans themselves say that no man can comprehend it, and that no man can instruct another in it. Thus, despairing of a solution of life's enigma, the Brahmans hit upon the idea that the universe is only a phantasm, a Dream of the Soul of the Universe, and as a consequence that the earth, with all that it contains, is nothing: this is pessimism. They imagined enormous eons of time, in the lapse of which the world grew ever worse and creatures were born only to suffer, to die, and either to awaken to suffering in the soul's migration, or to do penance in the unspeakable torments of hell. Now, as of all this the people could understand only what was said about the hell torments, the Brahmans contrived for them also a supreme deity under the same name as their own Soul of the Universe, Brahma, and for Brahma they provided a wife, Sarasvati. Brahma they made the creator, but the part played by him was only passive and the people, not content with such a do-nothing, paid more attention to other gods, specially to resplendent Vishnu and dread Siva. Long afterward the three gods were united in a sort of trinity, or, rather, were represented by a three-headed figure, which had neither temple nor sacrificial worship. Thus the Brahmans went on refining and refining in their theological speculations, while the people became divided into parties, Vishnuites and Sivaites, and the religion of the Hindus reached at last the state of debasement in which we find it today.

Before degeneration had gone so far Buddha, in the sixth century, B.C. endeavored to save the Hindu religion. Buddhism was not a new religion, only a reform of Brahmanism. Though it failed to strike root deep in its native soil, the more westerly countries of India, on the other hand it won a great following in farther India, Tibet, China, and Japan: it has since assumed a peculiar composite character by fusion with the ancient religions of those countries. It grew out of a monastic society founded by Siddhartha, afterward Buddha, surnamed the Perfect One. His doctrine was wholly ethical, and its profoundest principle was that only in complete renunciation of all things can man find safety and peace. Buddha himself was rather strict with postulants for admission to the society, so that in his time the teaching was in many respects a secret doctrine. But after the death of Buddha, when first himself, then several other Buddhas believed to have lived before him, and expected to come after him, had been raised to the rank of gods; and when to these had been added the Hindu gods and the gods of other peoples; the religion of the founder having thus degenerated into a polytheism, the learned began to interpret the original doctrine now in one sense, again in another, opinions differing on the question whether the Nirvana (literally, extinguishment) preached by Buddha meant Death and Nothingness, or a Blest State. Thus the Buddhism of the priests assumed a strong likeness to a secret doctrine, though we know not of any formal organization to that end.

11. Secret Leagues of Barbarous Peoples

EVEN AMONG SAVAGES so-called are found secret doctrines and secret societies of priests analogous to those of more cultured peoples. The priests of Hawaii, who in this respect perhaps rank highest among savage races, had a theory of their own regarding creation which shows great elevation of thought. The sorcerers, or priests, of savage races wherever they still remain, are banded in secret societies, which withhold from the people all knowledge of their tricks. The Angekoks of the Eskimos, the Medicine Men of the North American aboriginals, the Shamans of Siberia, as well as the sorcerers, however named, of African and other races, nearly all form close castes, hand down their pretended arts of weather-making, of healing disease, discovering thieves, counteracting spells, etc., to their successors, and prepare themselves for their office by undergoing strange tests and performing outlanish rites; they also wear fantastic togs. Among the Zulu Kaffirs the one who desires to become a sorcerer (usually a descendant of a sorcerer) gives up the customary mode of life, has strange dreams, seeks solitude, hops and jumps about, utters cries, handles serpents that other Kaffirs will not touch, at last receives instruction from some aged sorcerer, and is formally admitted by the assembly of those charlatans. There are also witches, or sorceresses, who go through a like form of consecration.

There exist also among savages other species of secret societies. In the Society Islands the chiefs, called Areoi or Erih, form an association, the origin of which they trace to Oros, god of war. They are divided into twelve classes under as many grandmasters, each class distinguished by a peculiar tattoo, the members are united by the firmest ties, show unbounded hospitality to one another, live without marriage, kill their own children, and refrain from all work. There are similar societies in Micronesia, called Klobbergoll, which assemble in special houses, and serve their chiefs in war as bodyguard. On the isle of New Britain (now a German possession, and named New Pomerania) there exists a secret society called the Duk-Duk, whose members, wearing frightful masks, care for the execution of the laws, collect fines, and inflict punishment on incendiaries and homicides. They are known to each other by secret signs, and outsiders are denied admission to their festivals under pain of death. In West Africa there are many secret societies whose members are distinguished by a chalk line, with which they are marked at their initiation. Their office is to pursue and punish criminals, and to collect the tribute. In each locality these associations possess houses for their special use, and their members are bound to the strictest secrecy. Thus even savages have their secret police and their privy tribunals.

PART SECOND

The Grecian Mysteries and the Roman Bacchanalia

1. Hellas

GRECIAN RELIGION IS worship of the beautiful. Its origin was as that of the other polytheistic religions: its basis was a personification of nature's forces and of the heavenly bodies, but in its evolution it differed essentially from the religions of the Oriental peoples, who had no sense for the beautiful, and who ascribed to their gods forms quaint, or unnatural, or hideous. In the dawn of their history the Hellenes did, undoubtedly, worship the forces of nature under the form of animals, especially of serpents. In time the human and animal forms were united, and there were deities with heads of animals or the bodies of horses (centaurs) or the hoofs of goats (satyrs). But the native genius of Greece asserted itself at an early period, and the figures of gods came by degrees to express the highest physical perfection with which they were acquainted the human form. True, the Hellenes, like the Easterns, forgot the astronomic and cosmic signification of their myths; but, whereas, for their neighbors oversea at least for the mass of the people the natural powers transformed into gods were simply fetiches existing only in the matter out of which they were made objects of dumb reverence or of mad terror;

for the man of Hellas they became changed into moral forces, into ideas which he represented to himself in beautiful forms that were to him not objects df fear at all, but beings with whom he might converse as with fellowmen, and of whom his poets sang as though of mortal heroes. Here we have the distinguishing characteristic of Grecian religious worship.

The Hellenes knew nothing of dogma, creeds, catechising, or revelation. In their eyes, if a man did but honor the gods as representing the groundwork of morality, he satisfied all the requirements of religion: the how, the when, the where, the how often, were matters left to the discretion of each one; and nobody else judged him concerning them. Of course, We must not apply our modern ethical yardstick to the principles of morality for which the gods stood sponsor, after the origin of the gods had been forgotten. The Greeks were, with regard to matters that we nowadays hold to be within the sphere of ethics, not at all scruple-ridden; and in truth we need to bear in mind their great services on behalf of the beautiful if we would look with some measure of allowance on their shortcomings with regard to virtue. In two points, specially straightforwardness (honesty, candor, truthfulness) and chastity, they left much to be desired; but what else was to be expected, seeing that in their gods, as in course of time they came to conceive of them mistakenly, they had by no means edifying exemplars of the moral principles to which those deities were supposed to give sanction. Nevertheless, history will, even to the Hellenes, forgive much, because they loved much.

Of so little obligation was the Grecian belief regarding the gods, that the several divisions of the Hellenic race were by no means agreed as to the number of the gods and their respective ranks. Of tne twelve gods of Olympus, one would be disowned here, another there. In one place greater honor would be paid to this god, in another place to that; the case is exactly that of the saints in Catholic countries today. Nay, local deities, e. g., Athene in Athens, often received more homage than Zeus, father of the gods and lord of the thunderclouds. The worship of the beautiful went even so far as to multiply gods, and to divide them among the different localities that possessed renowned statues of them: these statues then came to be regarded as distinct individuals, so that even a Socrates could be in doubt whether the Aphrodite Urania (Aphrodite in the sky) and Aphrodite Pandemos (the popular Aphrodite) were or were not one person. Nay, when the known gods did not suffice, they made gods that had no name: thus we find a "greatest" god, also "pure", and "reconciling", and "ruling", and, as we learn from the "Acts of the Apostles", "unknown" gods. And now as regards the character of all these deities: for the Greeks, who in all things studied the beautiful, they were neither monsters like the gods of Egypt, India, and Phoenicia, nor incorporeal spirits like the gods of the Persians and the Israelites, but human existences that never could die, mighty beings with human feelings, inclinations, and passions. The Greeks knew no Yahve: but then neither did they know any Devil. Their gods were neither faultless nor virtueless, just like the Greeks themselves. Of course there are to be found in Hellenic religion survivals from that period of mythology in which human and beast forms were mingled. This we see in the Centaurs, the Chimaera, the Minotaur, the Satyrs, etc.; but such beings were become merely figures in folk-tales, and there they enacted parts ranging from terror to farce: they no more received divine honors. And the same is to be said of daemons and malign spirits, relegated to the domain of superstition and the realm of poesy.

2. Hellenic Divine Worship

GRECIAN RELIGION WAS a function of state. Its adogmatism, it is true, abated the apprehension this fact might inspire for freedom of thought: but, on the other hand, religion came to be a cloak for the designs of political parties. Thus, for example, Socrates was put out of the way by the party opposed to him on the pretext that he had apostatized from the religion of the state. Heresy trials, except as stirred up by politicians, had no place among the Greeks. Philosophers and Initiates of the mysteries fearlessly expressed their convictions, however much opposed the same might be on one side or the other to the official theology: nay, comedy, and even the comedies of the tory Aristophanes introduced the gods in the most ridiculous and most disgraceful situations on the stage. It was enough for the state if the public worship of the gods, whose festivals were commanded, and whose sacrifices were prescribed by public authority, went on: for the state what individuals thought was of no consequence: the state cared neither for the upholding of positive nor for the putting down of negative beliefs. The public worship was regarded as a sort of legal transaction between the gods and the people: the gods were entitled to sacrifices, and the people to divine aid, and the two parties were held to make faithful exchange. Violation of temples and profanation of sacred things were, therefore, grievous crimes. One need not believe in miracles wrought by images of gods: but one must leave the images alone. And, inasmuch as the gods were officially recognized as vested with rights before the law, therefore, upon complaint - made and then only - denial of their existence, scoffing, and blasphemy were punished with banishment as the worst sort of crimes. Nor was there in this any fanaticism or any intolerance, simply an idea of right and wrong. That this is so is proved by the fact that there was no prohibition of the bringing in of alien gods or of the worship of such, provided only the customs of the land were not infringed; nay, alien gods, if their religion gained vogue, might be adopted into the religion of the state.

Such freedom of religion could, of course, exist only where no priestly caste existed, nor, in fact, any special priestly class. It was competent for persons in various walks of life to perform religious ceremonies. In the name of the state, the king (or other head of the government) "transacted business" with the gods, for example, conducted the sacrifices. Only in temples and other localities consecrated to divine worship were priests as such employed: but outside the walls of these they had nothing to do; for instance, they had nothing to do with men's consciences. In Hellas the priest had no privileges, no influence such as he had in Egypt, and priestly societies and priestly secret doctrine were out of the question. The service of some of the gods was conducted by women, and in the worship of certain deities only unmarried priests could engage; there were also certain other restrictions put on the priest's mode of life.

Among the Greeks religious ministration was no more restricted to certain places than to certain persons. The gods were everywhere, the highest inhabiting Olympus, others the sea, the netherworld, certain groves, trees, streams, mountains, grottoes, etc. Not in temples alone, but everywhere stood altars: in houses, in the streets, in forests. All consecrated places, whether temples or sacred groves, etc., were Asyla, places of refuge for offenders against law. The honor, done to the gods consisted in:

1. Invocation, comprising Prayers addressed, whether to the images of the gods or to their supposed abode, and pronounced low or loud or in song; Oaths, summoning the gods as witnesses of truth this at times degenerated into a species of Ordeal; Imprecations, calling on the gods to punish evildoers.

2. Votive offerings (anathemata), objects of all kinds laid at the feet of the gods' images: the offering might be an animal, fattened specially for the god, or it might be a person dedicated for life to the service of the god by himself, his father, or his master.

3. Sacrifices, mostly meat and drink offerings, but sometimes, living animals immolated to the gods, in atonement for sin, or to ratify treaties, or to obtain an intimation of the divine will or foreknowledge. In the earliest times human victims were immolated.

If religion consists in a belief in superterrestrial powers and in worship of them, so on the other hand, the belief in miracle has its root in the conviction that this worship is answered by action of the heavenly powers on the physical world. One instance of this action of the supersensual world is called Revelation. Here the Grecian religion was distinguished from other forms of belief in that it accepted no official standing revelation which everyone was required to believe, while it maintained the possibility of a revelation from the gods for emergencies. This belief was firmly held even by the most eminent Grecian philosophers, in particular by Socrates and the Stoics. And if the granting of prayers and the decision of questions by ordeals was a first feeble step toward revelation, the same mistaken belief led to still further degeneration of the religious idea in the forms of Seership, Oracles, and Conjuration.

Seership (in Greek, mantike, seer's art) was unintentional or intentional. Unintentional seership we see in dreams, and in trance. Intentional seership was practiced by interpretation of signs or omens (sign-reading). A "seer (mantis) was one who practiced sign-reading, whether self-deluded or simply pretending to be under divine inspiration. Folklore and history tell of famous seers who foretold the future from observation of the flight of birds, atmospheric phenomena, the position of constellations, and the entrails of animals; or who interpreted dreams and on occasion had ecstasies and visions. Then there were unprofessional practicers of the art who divined the future by other means; thus one would write the letters of the alphabet in a circle on the ground, lay on each letter a grain of corn, then let a cock pick up the grains, the operator meanwhile carefully noting the order in which the grains were picked up: this was known as alectromancy (Gr., alektor, cock; manteia, seership, divination).

Oracles are properly divinations obtainable only in particular places (as temples and other sanctuaries), and practiced only by duly qualified persons. There were several kinds of oracles, viz.:

1. Oracles from Signs. The most ancient oracle of this class was that of Zeus at Dodona, in Epirus, mentioned by Homer. The priests of the sanctuary at Dodona divined by observation of the rustling of the leaves of the sacred oak; they also cast lots on the altar, or questioned a sacred bronze basin.

2. Sententious Oracles. These were all sanctuaries sacred to Apollo, and were numerous in Hellas and Asia Minor. The most notable of them was one at Delphi. The! minister of the oracle of Delphi, a virgin priestess called the Pythia, while questioning the oracle sat on a tripod which stood over a crevice in the ground; thence issued a gas, and, intoxicated by inhaling this, the Pythia uttered words which the priests dressed up in verse or in sententious form.

3. Dream Oracles. Of these there were many, in sanctuaries dedicated to Ajklepios (Aesculapius, god of leechcraft) to which the sick were taken in order that through interpretation of the dreams they had on the spot they might obtain from the priests of Asklepios counsel upon the healing of their complaints. The most renowned of this class of oracles was at Epidaurus, in Argolis.

Conjuration, which developed into magic, was much used in ancient Greece, especially after the Greeks had come in contact with the Oriental world; but the gods and daemons concerned in this practice were all taken from foreign mythologies. People believed in conjuration of the weather, in transformation of men into animals, in love potions, etc., and employed magic formulas expressed in words that no one understood and that belonged to no earthly language.

3. The Hellenic Mysteries

SUCH WAS THE theology, and such the thaumatology* - image and reflection - of Grecian religion. The two elements constitute the popular religion, the religion of feeling, worship of the gods, as far as sensibility is concerned. But in the most ancient times there stood over against the popular religion (in Greece as in Egypt) a religion of priests, their Initiates, and Elect; over against the religion of feeling a religion of reflection; over against the naif, sensorial view, the sentimental, romantic, mystical one, the one which aims to acquire for belief an ethical side, and to subordinate that to faith. This phase of religion results from the mystic consideration that the individual is essentially different from the divine nature, subject thereto, and dependent on it; in short, it results from the idea of "alienation from God," toward which the superstitions of seership, oracles and magic were already showing the way. It was the impulse, given by

_____

* The orignal has Goetterglaube, belief in gods and Wunderglaube, belief in miracles, in allusion to the preceding section 2. Goetterglaube is of course equivalent to "theology," and if so, then Wunderglaube is equivalent to "thaumatology" from Greek thaumata, miracles, and logos, discourse.

reflection, to "seek the lost god" that led to the institution of mysteries in Greece: men were no longer satisfied with gods that were but man's equals. The mysteries contradict the origin of religion in feeling, they deny its dependence on art and the beautiful; they ponder and brood over the lost god, and are ever seeking him. They would subordinate life and all its interests to his service; they would regulate all man's acts, and hence morality, according to faith; they hold in contempt either man's power or his knowledge. The Grecian mysteries, indeed, borrowed from the popular religion its art, and turned it to account, but in them art was not cultivated for itself, and science was completely ignored. As science was free in Hellas and not tied to any priestly order, the mysteries could there render no service: there was nothing" for them to do. Of all the many philosophers of Greece, not one employed the doctrines of the mysteries In his system: not one showed any regard for them. The mysteries were then what they had ever been, and still are, to wit, self-introspection, interpretation of divine things, a mourning over the lost god, and search after the same, an endeavor for union with God, for grace and salvation, a sensible delight in the thought of a god suffering and dying, in meditation on the soul's state after death, on revelation, incarnation, and resurrection; and a representation of all these ideas in dramatic forms and ceremonies the main effect of which is to make an illusive and blinding impression on the senses.

Thus, the Grecian mysteries were the exact opposite of genuine Hellenism. Cheerfulness, joyousness, clearness of perception and of thought, absence of all mists and vapors, were the notes of your true Hellene: his statues of gods with their grand, bold, full, rounded contours to this day demonstrate this; and his superstition even took things just as they looked to him. On the other hand, gloom, ruefulness, a morbid, overweening, owlish phantastry, symbolry, mysticism, with every shallow trick of strained interpretation, and all the smugnesses of pharisaic piety are the earmarks of your mystic. On the one side day on the other night, there action here quest and longing, there fact here makebelieve, there alertness here moping, there a hearty meal off what is at hand here a hungering and thirsting after truth that never can be attained. The mysteries were therefore in every way ungrecian, outlandish, and abnormal. They had no fit place on Hellenic soil, nor in that age; they were the propaedeutic of a future age when one should come upon the scene who was to hurl Olympos, Okeanos, and Hades into the everlasting night of oblivion.

And yet from the difference between the Grecian mysteries and the ordinary life of the people it by no means follows that the Initiates did not find satisfaction, at least a partial satisfaction, in these mystic exercitations. The man who nurses the feeling of a want for something other than what his times and his surroundings afford, finds at the last in his very brooding the satisfaction of his need. Sentimental, romantic, fanciful, and mystical characters, therefore, must find uncommon delight in mysteries, while practical, clear-sighted, undistorted, and strictly logical minds are unmoved by them. Let us then listen to the testimony of two celebrated mystae, a Grecian and a Roman, both, it is true, living in a time when their respective nations had begun to decline. The tragic poet Euripides sings: "O blest is he whose fortune it is to have learned the divine initiations; he sanctifies his life." And Cicero (De Legibus II., 14) makes Marcus say to Atticus: "Of all the grand, and as I fain would think, the divine elements imported by thy Athens into human life, there is nought better than those Mysteries whereby we have been developed out of rudeness and savagery and trained to the human manner of life. And we, too, even as the Mysteries are called Initia (beginnings) so in them have found the principles (a play on words, "initia" and "principia," principles, being homonyms) of right living, and have learned not only to live joyously, but also to die with better hope." Then, as shadow follows light, he adds: "The thing I do mislike in the nocturnal rites, is told in the comic poets. Were such liberties permitted in Rome, what had not that infamous wretch (Clodius) done, who brought lewdness into the presence of certain sacred rites upon which 'twere sin even to glance unwittingly."

The Grecian mysteries were no monoply of the priests or of any other class: no man was excluded except such as by their life proved themselves unworthy of initiation. The origin of these mysteries is found in the rites of Purification and Atonement. ' In the earliest times the purifications were nothing but bodily cleansings prescribed to those who took part in religious ceremonies: later they took on a moral significance, as the sense of alienation from God gained ground. With the consciousness of sin, with the need of obtaining forgiveness, and, to that end, of knowing a deity free from all sin, and hence totally unlike man, mysticism begins and develops. Expiations came into vogue little by little, especially for bloodguilt-iness, and were used in the popular religion. These consisted of certain ceremonies in which the blood of animals and incense were employed; in the case of individuals such rites might lessen the punishment under mitigating circumstances; they might, in the case of cities and states, efface the stains of murderous crimes committed during revolts or civil strifes. In all the mysteries purifications and expiations played a great part. Whatever has been handed down with regard to these mysteries is found in the sections following.

4. The Eleusinian Mysteries

THE MOST ANCIENT, most celebrated, and most venerable among the Grecian mysteries were those instituted at Eleusis, in Attica, in honor of the goddess Demeter (called by the Latins Ceres) and her daughter Persephone (Proserpina), and later of a male deity also, known in the mysteries under the name of Iacchos; and though there is no affinity between the letters I and B, Iacchos came in time to stand for Bacchus. The original Iacchos would seem to have been a god in the people's religion, and this name is probably related to Jao (found in Jovispater, Jupiter) and to the Hebrew Yahve. Diodorus (I., 94) gives the name Jao to the God of the Hebrews; and an oracular utterance of the Apollo of Claros says:

Know thou that the highest of all the gods is named Jao,
and in Winter Aides, and Zeus in opening" Spring
then Helios in Summer, and once more Jaos in Fall.

The fact that Jaos was the harvest-god tended strongly to identify him with Bacchus, personification of the sun which ripens the grape; and, besides, Bacchus was allied to Demeter (originally Gemeter Earthmother) who was the patroness of husbandry. The name of the city, Eleusis, means in Greek "advent", and it commemorates the stay of Demeter there in the course of her wandering in search of her daughter: a like story is told of Isis in Egypt. In gratitude for their hospitality, Demeter bestowed on the people of Eleusis the bread-grain and the mysteries. From Eleusis the cult of the two deities spread all over Greece and part of Asia Minor, and in a modified form passed into Italy: in several places arose affiliated institutions resembling that at Eleusis, having the same festivals and the same secret cult; but Eleusis always held the supremacy. The buildings at Eleusis, in the pure Doric style, consisted of the temple of Demeter and the Mystic House, in which the secret festivals were held. They were connected with Athens by the "Sacred Way", a road flanked by temples and sanctuaries: in Athens itself was an Eleusinian building (Eleusinion) in which a portion of the mysteries was celebrated. In front o! the city gate toward the Piraeus was also a sanctuary dedicated to this cult, and furthermore an Eleusinion at Agrae. The buildings at Eleusis stood till the fourth century of our era: they were then destroyed by the Goths under Alaric, at the instigation of monkish fanatics.

The Eleusinia were always under the direction of the Athenian Government. When Athens became a democracy the functions till then performed by the King, as protector of the Eleusinia, devolved on the head of the executive, the Archons, who, therefore, bore the title Basileus (king) because the most important duties of the King had been concerned with Eleusis and its Mysteries. The Basileus was assisted by four councilors (epimeletae), of whom two were chosen from among the Athenians, and other two from the two Eleusinian gentes, Eumolpidae, and Kerytae. The report on the celebration of the Mysteries was always rendered to the Grand Council (Boule) of Athens, assembled in the Eleusinion. The function of priest in the institutions at Eleusis was always the exclusive privilege of the Eumolpidae and Kerytae. The chief of the priests was the hierophant, and with him was associated a hierophantess. Next to these in dignity were the torchbearer (daduchus), the sacred herald (hierokeryx), and the "altar-priest." These officials constituted the Sacred Council, which had the immediate direction of the mysteries.

It would be a great mistake to regard the Eleusinian Mysteries as a result of illuminism or rationalism. Rather were they an institution not less religious, not less faithful to the ancient traditions than the popular religion itself; with this difference only, that the latter contented itself with honoring the gods contemplated in the human form, while the mysteries emphasized the infinite preeminence of the divine nature over the human. Hence the mystic leligicri was guarded by the state authorities with the same zeal as the anthropomorphic religion of the vulgar.

No one saw in the one any danger to the other. The two forms of religion were branches of one tree, Pantheism, and herein only differed, that the one saw the Divine in all earthly things, the other sought for it there and strove for union with it. It is equally vain to look in the Eleusinia for either Rationalism or Monotheism. Monotheism, i. e., absolute severance of the earthly from the divine without hope of union, was a purely Oriental idea, quite incomprehensible to the Grecian mind: no ancient Greek writer ever dreamed of a creative demiurgus, in the Egyptian sense, nor of an angry and revengeful Yahve, like the Hebrews.

So great was the veneration for the Eleusinia among the Grecian states, that during the mystic festivals hostilities were suspended between opposing armies; and despisers of the mysteries, betrayers of the secret doctrine, and unbidden witnesses of the rites, were punished capitally or with lifelong banishment. In the year 411 E. C. the po.et Diagoras of Melos, who threw a figure of Herakles into fire, to put the hero to his thirteenth labor, and who had betrayed the mysteries, was banished for his irreligion. Even after the death of Hellenic liberty the Roman emperors took an interest in maintaining the Eleusinian sanctuaries. Hadrian sought and obtained the initiation, Antoninus erected edifices at Eleusis, nay, some of the early Christian emperors, as Constantius II. and Jovian, in their decrees forbidding nocturnal festivals made an exception of the Eleusinia; and after the destruction of the sacred buildings, the rites seem to have been still practiced.

The sum of all that is known of the doctrine taught at Eleusis is as follows: The myth underlying these mysteries was the rape, by Pluto, of Persephone, daughter of Demeter. Pluto, god of the netherworld in the popular belief, lord of the abode of the damned, in other terms, the personification of the sun that goes down in the west, hence of the sun of the nighttime, or of the Wintertime, carries off Persephone (personification of the world of plants), as she is plucking flowers (for as the cold season comes on the flowers wither and die), and takes her with him to the realm of shades, where she occupies the throne with him. But her mother Demeter, being, as goddess of the earth, the mother of the plant-world, and so too protectress of husbandry, wanders about lamenting, for indeed the earth loses its adornments, its loveliest features, in Winter. But at last the gods take pity on the hapless wanderer and bring about an agreement between her and Pluto, whereby Persephone is permitted to live in the uppenvorld in Summer, returning to the netherworld for Winter: here is signified the fecundity of the soil, and also the resurrection of man after his body has been dropped like a grain of corn in the earth. The union of Persephone with Bacchus, i. e., with the sun-god whose work is to promote fruitfulness, is an idea special to the mysteries, and means the union of humanity with godhead, the consummation aimed at in the mystic rites. Hence in all probability the central teaching of the mysteries was Personal Immortality, analogue of the return of the bloom to plants in Spring.

Now the festivals at Eleusis have reference to this myth. Of these festivals there were two, the Lesser Eleusinia in Spring (the month Anthesterion, March), when the ravished one came up out of the netherworld into the sunlight; these festivals were observed at Agrae; and the Greater Eleusinia in Autumn (the month Boedromion, October), when she must follow her sullen spouse again to Hades; they were observed at Athens and Eleusis. There was a preliminary celebration at Athens, and at Eleusis the high celebration. The preliminary solemnity lasted six days, Boedromion 15th to 20th. On the first day Initiates from every region wherever the Greek language was heard and Grecian hearts beat for the gods, assembled in the Poecile at Athens and there heard the order of the exercises proclaimed by the Hierophant, after his aides had first in a loud voice bidden the bloodguilty to depart. On the second day the mystae were summoned to go down to the seashore and to perform in the sacred brine the act of purification, requisite for a worthy observance of the solemnity. The remaining days were spent in performing the prescribed sacrifices, sharing in the sacrificial banquets, and making the customary solemn processions. On the sixth day came the grand Iacchus Procession, numbering thousands of mystae, of both sexes; these, issuing from the Sacred Gate, wended along the Sacred Road to Eleusis. They wore crowns of parsley and myrtle, and in their hands carried ears of corn, implements of husbandry and torches; for though the procession set out betimes it moved slowly, and reached the destination late, to celebrate the festival in the hallowed night. Iacchus himself was believed to be the leader of the procession, which was headed by his image in the form of a babe with costly toys and cradle. The line of march lay along the brink of the sea over the same flowery fields and grassy meadows of the Thriasian plains, which had been the scene of the rape of Persephone. The route was fourteen miles long, but to the participants! in their festive mood it was short, and besides they made frequent halts at the various sanctuaries on the way, practicing mystic rites and offering sacrifices. The rude wild chorus of the Hymn to Iacchus resounded, with intervals of animated dances and flute playing, and frequent shouts of Io, Iacchus, hail! But as we learn from the "Frogs" of Aristophanes, the processionists meanwhile indulged freely in merriment, chaffing their fellows, and making love to the women and girls. It was customary for women to make the journey in wains till a demagogue in the time of Demosthenes procured the abolition of this "privilege of the rich."

In the evening of the first day at Eleusis the mystae in common drank of the sacred potion Kykeon, by which Demeter was comforted at Eleusis during her wandering. It was a decoction of barley, wine, and grated cheese; to these afterward were added, one by one, honey, milk, certain herbs, salt, and onions. During the three succeeding nights the performing of the mystic rites and the initiations took place, the principal feature being the torch-processions representing Demeter's search for Persephone: during the day the Initiates seem to have fasted. After the initiations the festival was transformed into a scene of merriment and gymnastic competition. Probably the mystae returned to Athens processionally, and there the report on the festival was made to the Boule, whose non-initiated members had first to retire.

It was at these festivals that the rites of initiation into the Eleusinian mysteries were performed. Initiation was in two degrees, viz., that of the Lesser, and that of the Greater mysteries. Initiation into the Lesser mysteries took place during the preliminary festival, and that into the Greater mysteries either at the greater festival next ensuing or at the greater festival of a subsequent year. The Initiates of the Lesser mysteries were called Mystae, those of the Greater mysteries, Epoptae (those who have seen). It is probable that at both of the annual festivals the mystae took part only in the external ceremonies, and that only the Epoptae (or adepts) were admitted into the Sacred House at Eleusis, or inducted into the occult meaning of the festivals and ceremonies: this we infer from the exceedingly large number of the mystae.

The one who wished to be admitted to the mysteries had to apply to an initiated citizen of Athens, who by appointment of the authorities served as mediator between him and the priests: hence he was called Mystagogos, guide or sponsor of the postulant. As a rule the postulant was required to be a Hellene. Foreigners were admitted only when they were men of distinction, such, for example, as the Scythian philosopher Anacharsis. After the conquest of Greece by the Romans, Roman citizens stood on equality with Hellenes. There was no discrimination on the ground of sex. But no one stained with bloodguiltiness could be admitted.

Those who came up for admission to the degree of Epoptes, and who, as we suppose, had never entered the "Mystic House," were left to wander through its mazes, in profound darkness, meeting toils and hindrances and dangers. Then followed rites in which the courage of the candidates was subjected to the severest tests, so as to fill them with "fear and trembling and dread amaze." It is very probable that the terrors of the test were borrowed from the Grecian ideas of the netherworld. But after the darkness came brightness, after Tartarus Elysium, the Field of the Blest. The epoptes was suddenly gladdened by a miraculous light; smiling plains and meadows invited his footsteps, whence we must infer that the Mystic House was furnished forth with most ingenious scenic mechanisms, as trapdoors, magic lanterns, and other optical contrivances. Celestial voices and harmonies were heard, charming dances were executed, eye and ear were flattered by a display of the uttermost resources of Grecian art; and last came the most impressive scene of all, when the hierophant threw open' the door oi the inmost shrine of Demeter, bade the epoptae enter in, withdrew the veils from the images of the gods (whose true meaning was thus made known), and showed godhead in its most radiant splendor.

That the Initiates of the mysteries regarded their chances in the netherworld as better than those of the profane we learn not only from the sarcastic Aristophanes, who in the "Frogs" scores, the mystae as in myrtle groves they revel amid fluting and dancing, while the profane wander in darkness and mire, lapping water like dogs; but the serious-minded Sophocles tells us the same thing in a fragment quoted by Plutarch: "O, thrice blest the mortals who have witnessed these solemn rites, when they go down to Hades: for them alone is there life in the netherworld; for all others bootless affliction and misery."

5. The Mysteries of Samothrace

NEXT AFTER THE Eleusinia, the most ancient and renowned of the Grecian mysteries were thosfc of the Cabiri in the island of Samothrace. Who the Kabeiroi were men, or intermediate beings half human, half divine, also how many they were, no satisfactory conclusion has yet been reached on these points. But they date from very high antiquity, before the evolution of the several Grecian deities. In Egypt, according to Herodotus (Ill., 37), they were "worshiped as sons of Hephaestus (he means Ptah, god of Memphis); and were, like their father, figured in the shrine as Pygmies." That in the language of Phoenicia Kabirim means "the great, the mighty ones," is of no consequence, for here "great" is not used in the sense of bodily largeness. Neither is it any objection that in Greece the Kabeiroi are regarded as beings subordinate to the gods: for the earlier gods ever do take second place when new gods get footing. In early Egyptian mythology and religion the Cabiri were personifications of the stars; and the mysteries of Samothrace were originally an astromythology, though in time their astral significations were forgotten. From a remark of Herodotus (Il., 51) that the Athenians got from the Pelasgians inhabiting the island of Samothrace their custom of figuring Hermes with the Phallus (and everyone who has acquaintance with the secret cult of the Cabiri knows what that means), we are led to infer that in the Cabiric mysteries the reproductive forces of nature played an important part: the symbol of those forces, the Phallus, was employed by the nations of the East and from them passed to the Greeks, who originally had no leaning toward such obscene imaginings. The same inference is suggested by Juvenal's remark that in love affairs it was the fashion to swear by the Cabiri. For initiation into the Samothracian mysteries the novice was required to submit to a purification by fire and to fumigation, and to make a sort of confession. Plutarch tells of a Spartan who at his initiation inquired of the priest whether he should confess his sins to him or to the gods; and on the priest replying, "To the gods." "Then," said the penitent, "give way, I will tell it to the grodhead alone." Men, women, even children were initiated, and the professed received a purple band, which they wore around the body, in the assurance that by this means they would be safe against perils bv sea.

The Greeks used to tell of their fabled heroes, Orpheus, Agamemnon, Odysseus, etc., that they were Initiates of these mysteries; and Philip II. of Macedon and his queen Olympias, parents of Alexander the Great, underwent this initiation. There were Cabirian mysteries also in several other Grecian islands, and in several places on the continent, both in Greece and in Asia Minor.

6. The Mysteries of Crete

IN THE ISLAND of Crete were celebrated the mysteries of Zeus. According to the myth, the father of the gods and lord of all the world, to) foil the designs of his father Cronos, who had devoured all his other children, was, while yet a child, taken bv his mother Rhea to that island for refuge, and there guarded in a grotto of Mt. Ida and nourished with milk and honey by the people, who meanwhile, by dealing blows on each other's shields, kept up such a din as drowned the wailing of the babe. In Crete was also shown a sepulchre of Zeus. Regarding the Cretan mysteries we know this only, that in the Springtime the birth of the god was commemorated at the grotto and his death at the sepulchre, and that the while the young people (who represented the Curetae), in armor, with dance and sons: and with loud beating of cymbals and drums, enacted the story of the childhood of Zeus.

7. The Dionysia

AN ANCIENT NATIONAL cult among the Hellenes, into which a mystic element was imported from without, was the worship of Dionysos or Bacchus, i. e., of the sun as promoting the growth of the vine: its end was plainly to glorify the physical world, the material world, in all its manifestations of life and force. Hence the Bacchus cult is one predominantly materialistic, addressed to the sense of bodily pleasure, the appetite for food and the sexual desire; and yet, inasmuch as viticulture, like agriculture, is one of the factors of civilization, and as the Drama had its origin in these Dionysiac festivals, it cannot be denied that for many elements of our intellectual and spiritual culture we are indebted to this cult. Of the festivals of Dionysos some belonged exclusively to the popular religion, but others were connected with mysteries. Those of the former class had their chief seat in Attica, the others elsewhere. Of these non-mystic festivals of Dionysos in Attica there were seven, occurring in different months of the year, from the season of the vintage in Autumn till toward Spring , or while the new wine was in fermentation; and some of these festivals were held in the country, others in the city. On such occasions gymnastic sports of a ludicrous sort were carried on. as dancing on one leg, leaping on a leathern bag blown up with air and greased with oil outside, and trying to maintain equilibrium, etc. At the head of a procession composed of men and women of all ranks and degrees were borne the sacrificial implements, then followed the victim, a he-goat, and soon came the image of the Phallus, borne aloft with great pomp. So little did the Greeks possess of our peculiar sense of shame that they looked on this symbol as something entirely proper, not scrupling: even to sing satirical verses about it. After the sacrifice came jesting, banter, travesty, and with travesty pantomime, in which was enacted the history of the god, including" of course his fabled adventures. The stage had its rise in such festivals as these. The Spring festival, held in the month Anthesterion (month of flowers) was kept with special solemnity. It marked the time when the wine was racked off into the earthen pots. It was at this festival that the Basilissa (wife of the Basileus), accompanied by fourteen other women, entered the holy of holies of the ancient temple of Dionysos (at all other times women were forbidden to enter it), and there made a secret offering with mystic rites and vows.

But we have the genuine "mysterium" in the Dionysia Trietera, or triennial festival of Dionysos. Festivals of this class seem to have originated in Thrace, and hence among a people of Pelasgian stock. The spirit of the Thracians, which was naturally of a gloomy cast, but when their slumbering passions were awakened became wildly enthusiastic, seemed in these festivals, or rather these transports of moral frenzy, to pass into the persons of the lighthearted and selfcontrolled Hellenes. The mad extravaganza of this phenomenon in the history of man and his ways is seen in the Grecian hero-myth, which tells of the great singer Orpheus and Pentheus, king of Thebes, being torn limb from limb by the furious Maenades at festivals of Bacchus, the former because after the death of his beloved Eurydice he never more would hear of woman's love, and the latter because he had spied on the festivals. For these festivals were observed by women exclusively, who, drunken with wine, knew no restraints of reason or humanity: they were called maenades (madwomen) or Bacchae, and their festivals Orgia (orgies). The orgies were conducted on mountain sides or in mountain gorges at night under the light of torches, the fair participants, clothed in fawnskins, armed with the thyrsus wreathed with ivy and vine leaves, with hair disheveled, and, as the story goes, snakes tangled with its locks, or held in the bacchantes' hands. This festival, which occurred in the mild midwinter of Hellas, the time of shortest days and longest nights, continued over several days, during which the maenads, shunning all association with the male Sex, sacrificed, drank, danced, jubilated, made noise with the double-pipe and the brazen tymbal, nay, as the (manifestly improbable) story runs, with their own hands tore asunder the bull, symbol of the god, and destined to the sacrifice, and gloated over the victim's bellowing for pain. This feat was to show forth the death of Zagreus, one of the forms under which Dionysos appeared, and in which he was torn asunder by the Titans because he had been chosen by Zeus for his successor as ruler of the universe. The flesh of the bull was torn in shreds with the teeth by the maenads and devoured raw. Then the raving Bacchae invented a fable about the death of their god, and how he was lost and how he must be found again. But all the anxious searching was vain, and hope was centered in the finding again of the all-quickening Springtide. The observance of the Dionysia was not marked with these extravagances everywhere: in Attica such excesses were never seen. But Athenian women would attend the secret festival on Parnassus near Delphi, heedless of the mantle of snow on the summit.

8. The Roman Bacchanalia

THE WORST DISORDERS of Bacchus-worship, as practiced in Greece, would seem to have been equaled, or even surpassed, in the Roman Commonwealth. The historian Livy (xxxix., 8-20) compares the introduction of the cult into the city and its rapid spread to a visitation of plague. According to Livy the cult was brought to Rome from Etruria. In its Etruscan and Roman, form the worship of Bacchus was simply debauchery, under the thinnest possible cloak of religion. The festivals or orgies were at first observed by women; but a certain priestess of Bacchus, by command of the god, introduced the innovation of admitting men, and instead of three Bacchic festivals a year, instituted five festivals for each month; and whereas in Etruria the rites had been practiced in the day time, they now began to be held at night. From considerations of prudence the abominations of the Bacchanalia were guarded from public view by a hedge of ceremonial, and postulants for admission were required to practice for several days the strictest continence. But the term of probation being over, and the postulant admitted to the company of the Bacchanals, he or she found themselves surrounded by all conceivable incitements to the gratification of lust, in every way that the depraved instincts of man or woman had ever before, or perhaps has ever since contrived. According to Livy the Initiates of these mysteries numbered several thousand persons in the city, many of them belonging to the most distinguished families. In addition to the abominations of their secret meetings the Initiates were charged with conspiring against the commonwealth, with forgery of last testaments, with poisonings and assassinations, with the most revolting rapes. In the year 186 B.C. the Consul Spurius Postumius Albinus, having privately made inquiries into the doings of the sect, resolved to employ all the resources of the state for its suppression. The circumstances which led to this resolution were as follows: A youth of noble birth, Publius Aebutius, whose father was dead, was the ward of his stepfather, Titus Sempronius Rutilus. Now Sempronius had mismanaged the estate of Aebutius, and was unable to give an account of his guardianship, and therefore wished either rb have the youth put out of the way, or to get him under his power. The easiest way was by debauching him in the Bacchanalia. Aebutius's mother, devoted to her husband, pretended to the son that during his illness she had made vow to the gods to consecrate him to Bacchus in the event of recovery. Aebutius, nothing suspecting, told of this to one Hispala, a damsel of questionable reputation, with whom he had for some time been very intimate; but she entreated him for all the gods' sake not to have anything to do with the Bacchanalia: that she herself, as maid, had been initiated with her mistress, and knew what shocking deeds were done in those assemblies. Having promised her that he would not seek initiation, he made his resolution known to his parents, and was by them turned out of their house. Aebutius made complaint to his aunt Aebutia, and by her advice to the Consul Postumius. The Consul summoned Hispala to his presence, and from her, not without difficulty, for she feared the vengeance of the sect, learned what she knew of the proceedings at the secret assemblies. Then he brought the matter before the Senate, who gave to him and his colleague, Quintus Marcius Philippus, full powers for the suppression of the evil. Rewards were offered for trustworthy testimony, measures were taken to prevent the escape of guilty ones, and there were numerous arrests. Seven thousand persons in all were implicated, and all Italy awaited the outcome of the prosecution intently and with alarm. The ringleaders and a multitude of their accomplices were put to death, others were condemned to imprisonment or were exiled. Aebutius and Hispala received a large money reward; and Hispala furthermore was admitted to all the rights and privileges of a Romanborn freewoman, without prejudice from her previous disreputable career. A decree of the Senate forbade forever the holding of the Bacchanalia in Rome or in Italy. The decree provided that if anyone should consider such rites obligatory and necessary, or should think that he could not omit them without incurring the guilt of irreligion, he must lay the case before the Praetor Urbanus, and the Praetor must consult the Senate. If leave were granted in a senate having not less than one hundred members present, he (the person desiring to practice the worship of the god) might perform the rites, provided that not more than five persons were present at them, and that there was no common fund, nor any master of the ceremonies, or priest. All places sacred to Bacchus worship were ordered to be destroyed, "except there be here or there an ancient altar or consecrated image" of the god. But the prohibition of the Bacchanalia could not be kept in fcrce perpetually. The abuses of the Bacchus cult went on unchecked outside of Italy, and by degrees sprung up again even on Italian ground, till they reached the pitch of absolute shamelessness in imperial times, as when the notorious Messalina, and other imperial strumpets, celebrated the most shocking orgies in the very palace.

9. Debased Mysteries from the East

NEAR AKIN TO the Dionysos cult, in many points coinciding with it, as well as with one another, and also, like the depraved forms of that cult, surreptitiously introduced from the Orient into Greece and then into Rome, we have the mysteries of the mother of the gods Rhea or Cybele, those of Mithras, and those of Sabazios cults and deities that were finally grouped together by the Orphic sect, of which anon.

Rhea was sister and spouse of Cronos and mother of the king of the gods, Zeus, whom she took to Crete, as we have already seen, to savd him from his father's violence. She is the Earth deified, like her mother Gaea, and is therefore often confounded with other goddesses answering to the same element, especially with the earth-goddess Kybele (Cybele), named after Mt. Kybelos or Kybela in Phrygia, who, according to Phrygian myth, when exposed by her father, King Maeon, was suckled by panthers and brought up by herdsmen, and afterward fell in love with the youth Attis (afterward Papas, both meaning "father"), of whom she exacted a vow of chastity as her priest. Attis having broken his vow for the sake of a lovely nymph, the goddess in her wrath deprived him of reason, and in his frenzy he castrated himself. The goddess thereupon ordained that in future all her priests should be eunuchs. There are countless other stories told of Attis and Cybele, but they nearly all agree in telling that Attis with manhood lost life also, and that Cybele, frenzied by grief, thereafter roamed about disconsolate and despairing. Like Dionysos, she was always followed by a long human and animal retinue (the moon with the starry host!), and rode in a wain drawn by lions, a mural crown circling her veiled head; while Attis was always represented as an ecstatically sentimental youth beneath a tree, with the Phrygian cap on his head and wearing white bag trousers. In Phrygia Cybele was worshiped under the form of a simple stone. The scene of her feats and sufferances was laid in gorgeous wildernesses, in fragrant groves, among the hillsides and glades known to the shepherd and the hunter. As in Dionysos we see the wild abandon of a jovial spirit, so in Cybele we have the recklessness of a soul weary of life; hence at her festivals all centered in the loss of Attis, and a pine tree was felled, because his catastrophe took place under a tree of that species. All this was accompanied by a hubbub of wild music, and the winding of horns on the second day announced the resurrection of Attis. In the ecstasy of joy the participants were seized by a wild frenzy. With shouts and cries, their long locks disheveled, and in their hands bearing torches, the priests danced and capered like madmen, roaming over hill and dale, mutilating themselves, even emasculating themselves (as the myth required), and bearing about, instead of the figure of the Phallus, the proofs of their compliance with the precept of the goddess. The cult of Cybele was for the first time formally organized as a mystic society in Rome, but the orgiast frenzy clung to it at all times. The processions did not move with measured steps and in orderly ranks, as those of other cults, but the Initiates ran in confused troops, shouting their religious songs, through hamlets and towns, armed with curved blades, tokens of castration. At Rome the priests of Cybele were called Galli, that is, cocks. In the time of the emperors purifications in the blood of bulls and rams were introduced, apparently in honor of the Springtide, when the sun enters the constellations Taurus and Aries, and the vegetable powers of nature reappear. That is the theme of all the ancient mysteries, and indeed of all mysticism from the earliest times to this day. In all of them the vicissitudes of the vegetal world, its sickening, decline, and death in the Fall, its new-birth and resurrection in the Spring, are allegorized into the sufferances, the death and the resurrection of a god. Out of this nature-cult arc little by little developed the feeling of alienation of man from God, the quest for the god, the finding of him, and the consequent reunion, with the result of strengthening the assurance of the soul's immortality. The excess of sensual delight found in the Bacchanalia, and the extreme renunciation of delights by the castrate ministers of Cybele, are only variations of one same theory of human life.

Now, as this suffering godhead which was the prime inspiration of all these sensualists and adventurers was an importation from Thrace in the form of Zagreus-Dionysos, and from Phrygia as Attis, so was Mithras an importation from Persia. Among the ancient Persians Mithras was the light, conceived as a personality, and hence was the highest manifestation of the good god Ormuzd, while the darkness represented Ahriman, the evil god. Hence the worship of Mithras is worship of the light, and, therefore is the purest cult that heathendom could imagine; in the later times of the Persian empire Mithras-worship was combined with sun-worship, and Mithras, as sun-god, found a place in the religion of European peoples. In those later times also came belief in a female deity called Mithra: but Mithra was unknown to the primitive Persians, and the name was a transformation of the Babylonian Mylitta, the moon-goddess. Of the existence of secret cults among the Persians we know nothing whatever, hence nothing about any mysteries sacred to Mithras. To the Greeks Mithras was unknown, but in the latter days of the Roman empire, among many mysteries those of Mithras made their appearance and even gained great pre-eminence, as is proved by numerous monuments still extant. These monuments all consist of representations in stone of a young man in a cave, wearing the Phrygian cap, in the act of slaying with a dagger a bull; all around are figures of men and animals, all symbolical of constellations, as the scorpion, dog, serpent, etc. The groups have been variously interpreted, but the most probable view is that the youth stands for the sun-god, who, on subduing Taurus (in May), begins to develop his highest power.

The mysteries of Mithras, like their symbolic representation in the monuments, were celebrated in grottoes, and had for their original end worship of light and of the sun, and the glorifying of the sun's victory over the darkness; but this lofty idea gave way, in these as in other mysteries, to vain reveries and subtleties; and in the corrupt age of the Roman emperors it had, in all probability, some very ugly developments, such as were seen in the Bacchanalia. The rites of initiation were more elaborate than in the Grecian mysteries. The postulants were subjected to a long series of probationary tests eighty in all, it is supposed which grew more and more severe till they became actually dangerous to life. Among the initiatory rites the principal ones were a baptism and the drinking of a potion of meal and water. Admission to the highest secrets was reached through several degrees, probably seven, each having its special ritual and its special doctrines. At times the Initiates were required to fast, and those of the highest degree were vowed to celibacy. Such abstinences were all unknown to the ancient Persians; on the other hand human sacrifices came in. with Mithraism from the East, and, despite the decrees of the Emperor Hadrian, such sacrifices were offered in the Mithras cult. Commodus with his own hand immolated a man to Mithras, and his successors,, in particular the monster Heliogabalus, carried the abomination farther, and made of the pure god of light a bloodthirsty Moloch. Nay, after the empire had been christianized, Julian the apostate consecrated in Constantinople a sanctuary to Mithras. But after the death of Julian the cult was forbidden in the empire (A. D. 378) and the grotto of Mithras at Rome destroyed. Coins were struck in honor of Mithras, and he was honored with public inscriptions in the words, Soli Invicto (to the unconquered sun); a festival also was instituted in his honor, called the Natal Day of the Unconquered Sun: it fell on December 25th and was publicly observed: the same day was in Persia New Year's. In the monuments already mentioned, which commemorate the worship of Mithras, are seen inscribed alongside the neck of the bull the words "Nama Sebesio," supposed by some to be a mixture of Sanskrit and Persian, and to signify Worship to the Pure; but in these words we have an allusion to a new god and his cult. In the latter Graeco-Roman time, when the mystery craze possessed all minds, a combination of Zagreus, Attis, and Mithras was made, and the result was dubbed Sabazius. The name Sabazius is given by sundry writers to various gods and sons of gods, and the word comes probably from the Greek verb Sabazein (to smash, break to pieces), indicating the wild disorder of this cult. Diodorus gives this name to the inventor of the use of oxen in ploughing, other authors confound Sabazius, as discoverer of the vine, with Bacchus. There existed in Greece a public and a secret cult of Sabazius, both resembling the Bacchic cult, with ludicrous dances, uproarious singing, and loud thumping of cymbals and drums. The orator Aeschines, rival of Demosthenes, was an enthusiastic Sabazist. At initiation into the Sabazian mysteries the postulant had snakes dropped into his bosom, was robed in fawnskin, his face daubed with clay, then washed in token of a mystic purification; he was now to exclaim: From, evil I am escaped and have found the better. There was much hocuspocus and absurd jugglery withal, but the real object was to give opportunity to Initiates of both sexes to indulge in the most shameless gluttony and lewdness. The priests of this cult were the most impudent of mendicants. Aristophanes exhausted on Sabazius, the "trumpery god," all the resources of his caustic sarcasm.

And thus in time, as Grecian philosophy began to undermine the thrones of the Olympian gods, and to banish the phantoms of the netherworld, and the educated people to look on the fair forms of the world of gods as fictions of imagination; simultaneously the mysteries began to be stript of the glory of a heavenly origin, and it was seen that their rites were not only of the earth earthy, but as time went on, that they were become mischievous: yet the Initiates, lost to all shame and all moral sense, persisted nevertheless in their sacred hypocrisy, till heathendom as a whole had passed out of the bloody, hideous night of the gods.

PART THIRD

The Pythagorean League
and Other Secret Associations

1. Pythagoras

THE MYSTERIES SO far considered had for their foundation the worship of the gods. They were accessible only to the initiated; but candidates for admission were not carefully selected; and in Athens anyone of fair repute was eligible for initiation into the Eleusinia. Nor do we discern in the mysteries any "end" aimed at any idea to be realized, any thought to be embodied in action. From all that we can learn with certainty regarding the mysteries, their object was either simply to illustrate or interpret certain ideas (such as we have already characterized) by means of elaborate ceremonies; or in their state of decay and degeneration to minister to unbridled sensuality. For this reason we cannot regard the mysteries we have been studying as true "secret societies," for the distinctive note of such societies is that they make a special selection of their members, and have a specific aim. The earliest historic instance of such a secret society is afforded by the Pythagorean League.

The great philosopher Pythagoras was a sort of Grecian Moses or Jesus, a Messiah to whom were ascribed supreme wisdom, far-reaching plans, ideas of worldwide reform; who proclaimed new ideas, quite unknown in the previous history of his nation, and preached a new system of nature and of life; who gathered around him disciples that swore in his words and pursued peculiar ends disconnected from the interests of this world; who on that account was, with his disciples, persecuted, imprisoned, and martyred for his principles, by a world which deemed itself outraged; and whose history, because of its extraordinary character, became deeply incrusted with fable and fiction, till at last there was left only a figure in which, if not quite impossible, it is certainly difficult, to decide how far it conforms to the truth.

Pythagoras was born in the island of Samos B.C. 580 or, according to some authorities, 569. He is represented as of distinguished presence and imposing stature. That he possessed uncommon intellectual power is shown by his scientific discoveries and by his wonderfully organized discipleship. Even in his youthful years, it is related, he busied himself with his favorite sciences, mathematics and music, the mutual relations of which and their mutual influence he is, in fact, believed' to have discovered. His years of study ended of them we have no definite knowledge his years of travel followed. And whither should a man in his day. athirst for wisdom, direct his steps if not to the land of wonders on the Nile, where the veiled image at Sais sat enthroned, and where the mystic silence of the priests suggested to the visitant treasures of knowledge hidden in their temples? Whether the counsel to visit Egypt came from Thales, first of Grecian philosophers to seek the land of Nile tradition, which gives the glamour to everything, likes to bring renowned men together; whether Polycrates, tyrannos of Samos, commended him to his friend the Pharao Amasis of this we have no certainty, though the thing is not improbable, for the chronology is consistent, especially when \ve bear in mind the discrepancies between authors as to the year of Pythagoras's birth: at all events, Pythagoras voyaged to Egypt. The serious difficulties he met with on the part of the priests of Osiris, then not so complaisant as they afterward became, we have described already when giving account of the Egyptian mysteries. By hook or by crook he obtained, whether at Thebes, Heliopolis, or elsewhere, we know not, indoctrination in the theology of the One God. But of what avail could that be to him? His countrymen had already fashioned their own ideas of the divine nature. They based their theology on nature and spiritualized nature: the Greeks knew nothing of an impassable gulf yawning between god and world; for them these two were bound together and pervaded each other: to such a people one could not preach an "architect of the universe." Pythagoras, therefore, fain would communicate to the Greeks of the Egyptian wisdom whatever seemed adapted to their use; and he the more willingly complied with the Initiate's oath to observe lifelong silence regarding what he had seen and heard in the temples, as his countrymen would not have understood even a monotheism specially designed for them. For the Greeks the intimate association between god and universe was not only an idea, it was flesh of their flesh, bone of their bones: it was gloriously immortalized in the imperishable masterworks of their architecture and sculpture, and surely Grecian sculptors must not go to school in Egypt to learn how to carve cows' horns and hawks' heads. Nevertheless, the doctrine of the one god must necessarily have impressed the mind of Pythagoras deeply: he must have recognized therein a profound philosophy, though it may not have satisfied him completely; and hence it was his task, as it was the task of Plato and of all other Greeks initiated in the Egyptian mysteries', to expound the doctrine of the one god according to Grecian ideas to couple Oriental wisdom with Grecian fancy.

The traditional story represents Pythagoras as tarrying in Egypt when the Persian king Cambyses conquered the country, and tells how that tyrant had the Grecian philosopher deported, with other captives, to Babylon, where Pythagoras became acquainted with Zoroaster, and to his knowledge of the Egyptian wisdom now added a mastery of the wisdom of the Persians. Pythagoras was undoubtedly contemporary with Cambyses; but the time of Zoroaster is so undecided that the story must be regarded as fiction.

When he returned to his native Samos, purposing to set up as a master, he found to his chagrin that independent science is a plant that does not thrive under tyranny, and, compelled by force of circumstances to change his abode, he settled in Magna Graecia Southern Italy. On the eastern coast, in what became afterward Calabria, were two Achaean cities, Sybaris and Crotona. Pythagoras intended at first to make his home in Sybaris, but Sybaris could be no congenial home for such a philosopher. Crotona afforded a more promising field for his work, and there the labors of Pythagoras before long were abundantly rewarded. The Greeks ever were eager for novelties (novarum rerum cupidi), and whoever brought anything new was welcome. As yet, philosophy was a thing unknown among the Crotoniats; therefore they received its apostle with gladness and enthusiasm. Pythagoras commenced by giving public lectures in the council hall; as these awakened more and more interest every day, the philosopher was employed by the authorities to give counsel to the citizens; he then established a school, thus adding to his public functions the duties of a private instructor. Pythagoras used three agencies in his work, viz., his Doctrine, his School, and the League instituted by him.

The Doctrine of Pythagoras holds a distinct place among the philosophic systems of the Greeks. With regard to the opposition existing between the spiritual and the physical, and the uncertainty and obscurity that reigns as to the relations between them and the true constitution of each, the doctrine solves all difficulties by the theory that Number is at once the form and the substance of all things. All things consist of Numbers, corporeal elements as well as spiritual (mental, or intellectual) forces, and henceforth Pythagoras's philosophy became mathematics. But the silly tricks with numbers that occupied the ingenuity of later Pythagoreans possess no interest for us. It is probable that the master contented himself with the undeniable fact that the matter and essence of things rest on mathematical relations a view of great profundity, considering the age in which the philosopher lived. To Pythagoras and his school are credited the distinction of numbers into even and odd, the decimal numeration, square and cubic numbers, as also the famous Pythagorean theorem, the triumph of geometry.

Pythagoras brought music into closest relation with mathematics. As in numbers he recognized the most perfect "harmony," so he must needs regard harmony of sounds as a necessary part of the harmony of numbers. By this association he became the discoverer of our present scale of seven musical notes the octave. But his idea of harmony found most perfect embodiment in the universal creation, and in astronomy he was the first to surmise that the earth does not stand still, but has a revolution around a centre; hence, that it is not the principal existence in the universal frame of things, that all things 'do not exist for its sake, that Earth is not twin sister of the Heavens. True, Pythagoras had no idea, nor could have in the then existing lack of astronomical instruments, how the heavenly bodies were related: that was the discovery of Copernicus and Kepler. He took for the mid-point of the universe a "central fire" out of which were formed all the heavenly bodies this the seat of the power that sustains the world, the centre of gravity of all things. Around this central fire revolve the "ten" heavenly bodies farthest off the heaven of the fixed stars, then the five planets known to antiquity, then the sun, moon, earth, and lastly the "counter-earth", which revolves between the earth and the central fire. Revolving along with the earth, the counter-earth is always interposed between the earth and the central fire: light comes to the earth only indirectly, by reflection from the sun. When the earth is on the same side of the central fire as the sun we have day; when it is on the other side, night. Thus, Pythagoras may be said to have surmised a central sun, though his theory did. not contemplate the actual sun as that centre. He was also the first to explain the vicissitudes of the seasons by the obliquity of the earth's axis to the ecliptic. Further, he discovered the identity of the morning and evening star. His school held the moon to be the home of fairer and larger plants, animals, and human creatures, than those Of earth. In accordance with his doctrine of harmony he ventured to express the bold idea that the heavenly bodies by their movement produce tones which together constitute a perfectly harmonious music the music of the spheres. We do not hear this harmony, being so wonted to it.

Nor did he fail to apply to the soul of man this doctrine of harmony. By harmony the opposition between reason and passion was to be reconciled. But as this consummation is never to be achieved as long as soul and body are tied together, the sage of Samos regarded this union as a measure of probation, destined to endure till man shall have made himself worthy of liberation from the same; and when he fails of this during, his span of life, then his soul must migrate through the bodies of other men and animals till it shall become worthy of leading, in a higher region of light, an incorporeal life of purity and perfection. His disciples, furthermore, cherished the fantastic idea that the master was able to recognize in another body the man whose soul had transmigrated into it. That Pythagoras himself ever pretended or believed that he himself was in his fifth metempsychosis, or that he was son of Apollo, or that he had a golden hip, or a golden thigh, are either ridiculous extravaganzas of imaginative disciples or the sarcastic stories of his enemies. But noble and beautiful are the conclusions which he draws from his doctrine regarding purity of life, namely, the moral precepts which he laid down for the attainment of the supreme end. They required an absolutely stainless life. Pythagoras enforced the duty of reverence toward parents and the aged, fidelity in friendship, strict self-examination, circumspection in all our acts, patriotism, etc. Further, his disciples were required to be cleanly of body and cleanly in attire; they were to abstain from all "unclean" food, especially flesh meat, and from intoxicating liquors, and hence to live on bread and fruits only, but beans were an exception to this rule; for some not fully explained reason beans were an abomination to the Pythagoreans. And that which was unfit as food was unfit also as matter for offerings to God: for the god our philosopher reverenced was a god of light and purity. His clear intellect rejected polytheism, though what his view of the unity of godhead was we know nothing save that his faith was an eminently pure and exalted one.

2. The Pythagoreans

THE LIFE OF Pythagoras was devoted entirely to his School and his League. The School was the seedfield or seminary of the League, and the League was the practical application of the School's teaching. Thus the School was preparatory to the League, whose members were educated in the School.

Pythagoras enjoyed the boundless reverence of his disciples: when they wished to assert any proposition as indisputably true, they would say, He himself said it (Gr., autos ephe, Lat, ipse dixit). And this reverence for the Master increased as in time the School was changed from an open institution to a secret one. For at first everybody, even the most learned and most eminent of the citizens, attended the lectures of the Philosopher. Those who were simply hearers of the lectures were called Acusmatics (akusmatikoi). But those who were of proper age for receiving a further education, and who had leisure to devote themselves to learning, were afforded opportunity for pursuing higher studies under the personal direction of Pythagoras, and were known, not as simple Hearers, but as Students, or Mathematici. These were the nucleus of the Pythagorean sect. This class of disciples having grown considerably in numbers and influence, it became possible for Pythagoras, helped by the contributions that flowed in, to erect for his academy a special building, or, rather, group of buildings, in which he and his disciples might live secluded from the influences of the outerworld. This institution, called the Koinobion (coenobium, place where people live in community) was a world in itself, and embraced all the conveniences of plain living gardens, groves, promenades, halls, baths, etc., so that the student did not regret the hurlyburly of the world without. Henceforth the Acusmatici, or Acustici, were no longer persons of all classes and degrees, admitted to attend the lectures, but the newly admitted pupils, who received instruction in the elements of the sciences, and were preparing themselves for the higher studies. They had to observe strict silence and to yield blind obedience, and were not permitted to see the Master's face: at the lectures a curtain screened him from view. The advanced students were admitted behind the screen, and hence were called esoterikoi (esoterici, insiders): those before the curtain, exoterikoi (exoterici, outsiders). To gain admission to the esoteric class a pupil was required to spend from two to five years in study, and then had to undergo severe tests. If a student failed to answer the tests he was rejected: but if he passed successfully, he was no longer required to observe silence and to be content with listening only: he might now see the Master face to face, and under his direction might pursue a study chosen by himself, as philosophy, mathematics, astronomy, music, etc. Gymnastic exercise was practiced diligently, and was made the cornerstone of the Pythagorean therapeutic, which for the rest was a science of dietetic.

These approved and tested students formed the core of the celebrated League, which, in conformity with the division of the pupils in the School, comprised Exoterics and Esoterics. The Esoteric members of the League were, no doubt, the students admitted to the higher classes, as well as the graduates of the school: probably the number of these never exceeded 300. But to become an Exoteric member of the League, anyone was qualified who was a follower of the Philosopher, and who was ready to live according to his teaching and to spread the knowledge of the doctrine abroad: of these there may have been several thousand. Their mode of life was left to their discretion, while, on the contrary, the Esoterici were bound by strict rules. They lived in the Coenobium, always wore clothes of white linen, washed and bathed daily in cold water, at their common board abstained from the meats and drinks forbidden by the Master, and put in practice his doctrine. They divided the day among their various duties, meditating, mornings, how they might employ the hours most profitably, and evenings questioning themselves how their good resolutions had been kept. Harmony, that foundation-idea of the Pythagorean doctrine, was the lodestar of their lives. They studied to be just toward all men, toward the erring strict and kind-ly, faithful to friends and yokemates, to the law submissive, toward the unfortunate charitable, temperate in their pleasures; to keep their plighted word, and in their behavior to set a good example to all men. The League is said to have comprised several sections, but whether the sections were "degrees" rising one above another, or whether they were co-ordinate branches, is not clear. We hear of Mathematici, who devoted themselves specially to the sciences, of Theoretic!, who were professors of ethics, of Politici, concerned with government, of Sebastici. whose province was religion. The religion of the Pythagoreans seems to have been compounded of doctrines of the ancient popular religion of the Greeks, of the mysteries, and of the monotheism of the Egyptian priests; and it had a secret cult, with elaborate ceremonial of initiation, the purpose of which, how-ever, was to enforce the teaching of the Master.

The political principles of the Pythagoreans favored a trans-formation of the Dorian oligarchism into an aristocratism of culture. Democracy they hated. Their aim was to acquire for themselves powerful influence in the the state, to fill the public offices with their own members, and to administer government according their Master's ideas. As matter of fact, they appear to have attained these ends fully or approximately in Crotona, Locri, Metapontum, Taren-tum, and other cities of Magna Graecia. There is no doubt that the secrets that the Pythagoreans were sworn to keep had reference to these political aims. To bar out the uninitiated the members are said to have had a badge, a five-pointed star (pentagrammon, pentalpha) and to have employed a symbolic form of speech, by means of which they concealed their secrets under cover of apparently trivial words, or words not to be understood by outsiders.

But the League of the Sage of Crotona, after a glorious, though brief, ascendency, had a tragic end. The cities of Magna Graecia had grown rich by commerce, and with wealth and ease had come great corruption of manners. In Sybaris the lower classes of citizens artisans and shopkeepers rose in revolt, and five hundred patricians were banished, their property seized by the people, and the popular leader Telys administered the government in their stead. The exiles took refuge in Crotona, and there, according to Grecian custom, sitting around the altar in the agora, or market place, implored the aid of that city, then ruled by the Pythagoreans. Thus for two reasons the rulers of Crotona were objects of hate to the tyrannos of Sybaris: they were the enemies of democracy, and they were protectors of the exiled oligarchs. He, therefore, demanded of Crotona surrender of the fugitives. The demand having been refused (at the urgent instance of Pythagoras it is said), war followed. A desperate battle was fought, and the Crotoniats, though inferior in number, were victorious (510 B.C). Sybaris fell into their hands, and was looted without mercy, and the town leveled with the ground: in fact, a stream was made to flow through the once magnificent city.

This atrocious deed, which though no consequence of Pythagorean teaching, was nevertheless a consequence of Pythagorean exclusiveness and Pythagorean contempt for the people, had its nemesis. The democratic spirit, so mortally offended, took an equally atrocious revenge. In Crotona, too, as before in Sybaris, the democracy took action, and demanded a division of the conquered Sybarite territory among all the citizens of Crotona, and equal suffrage for all in the election of the rulers. At the head of the democracy stood Cylon, an enemy of the Pythagoreans. The aged Master, because of the hostility manifested toward him personally, was obliged to flee from the scene of his great labors. It is supposed that he died at Metapontum, hard on a hundred years old. In Crotona the strife of parties went on. The government unwisely rejected the demands of the democrats, and thereupon, about the middle of the fifth century B.C. the storm burst. The rage of the oppressed and despised people was vented first upon the Pythagoreans, a great number of whom were assembled in the house of Milo. The house was taken by storm, the assemblage butchered either on the spot or in flight, and their property distributed among the people. Aristocracy was also overthrown in Tarentum, Metapontum, and Locri. The Pythagorean League was annihilated, and its religious and political labors disappeared, leaving no trace.

3. The Orphici

THE SCATTERED FRAGMENTS of the Pythagorean League attached themselves to another association, that of the Orphici, named after the fabled singer Orpheus. This curious association, a fantastic compound of the mysteries and Pythagorism, is rightly credited to Onomacritus, apostle and reformer of the Eleusinian andDionysian mysteries, who lived in the time of the Athenian tyrannos Pisistratus: he was high in the favor of Pisistratus, and enjoyed much celebrity. By some of his contemporaries, men of sense and not easily imposed on, he was suspected of palming off his own compositions for poems of Orpheus (who never existed); but probably he did this without intent to deceive, but simply because of his irresistible passion for the mummery of secret societies and mysteries, This adventurer and mystic, who understood very well the meaning of the mysteries and the uses to which they could be turned, was one of the first to speak out the thought hidden in them: that man was born in sin and fallen away from God, and that he cannot be saved till grace shall be afforded him. His doctrine was just Pietism, with this exception, that instead of "the lord Jesus" we have here the god Dionysos, or the Iacchos of the mysteries, or Orpheus. Such inane babblement as this, and such doctrines as that the soul of man is confined in the body as in a prison, that the world is for it a vale of tears and a place of banishment, that it is pining and longing to return to its true home, Heaven, are an offense to the joyous spirit of Greece, an outrage against her religion of beauty, truth, and virtue, the last blow dealt at Grecian art and science. The outcome of them was a tedious, voluminous "Orphic literature" consisting of mythological poems full of mysticism and sentimentality.

The Orphic societies were not, like the mysteries, great assemblages of people in temples, but, after the Pythagorean pattern, secret schools or clubs; and they followed, at least ostensibly, the Pythagorean rule of life, abstaining from fleshmeat, beans, and wine; but with this they coupled two cults in themselves incompatible, that of the ideal god Apollo, and that of the sensual deity Dionysos. But being stript of the semi-public and official chraracter attaching to the mysteries, and of the philosophic dignity of the Pythagorean sect, the Orphic societies became simply nests of swindlers and mendicants; and vagabond priests, Orpheotelestae, admitted to their ridiculous degrees, for a consideration, every credulous and marvel-gobbeting postulant; there were even victims who had themselves with wife and children initiated every month. Other tricksters combined the Orphic cult with the Phrygian cult of Cybele, mother of the gods, and with that of Sabazios: these were known as Metragyrtae (mother-beggars) or Menagyrtae (monthly beggars). These and their like were regular mountebanks, giving out that they had the power of curing the insane, their method being to dance and caper around the patient to the sound of timbrels, the while flagellating themselves: for this they took up a little collection. One of these metragyrtae was capitally punished at Athens in the middle of the fifth century B.C.: but the judges, seized by remorse, questioned the oracle, and got response that in atonement they should build a temple to the Great Mother: thereupon the followers of the dead juggler were set free. A priestess of Sabazios, Ninus by name, was also put to death for brewing philters: she was the one sole victim of witchcraft trials in all antiquity. Thus did the Orphic sect in Greece degenerate to the same low estate as the mysteries, despised by all honest and enlightened men.

But both! the mysteries and the Orphic as well as Pythagorean societies were links in a chain of phenomena that reached all through Grecian antiquity, indicating plainly a reaction against the popular religion, and an effort to introduce essentially different religious views views which in aftertimes, in an improved form, were to triumph definitely over the Olympian gods.

4. Mysterious Personages of Ancient Times

IN ANTIQUITY WE are able to distinguish three religious systems, viz., polytheism, monotheism, mysticism. The first was a deification of nature: and as nature manifests herself in various forces, the religion, too, had to postulate a multitude of deities. This is the system of the Oriental and Graeco-Roman popular religion; and in these its two branches it is again differentiated by the fact that on the one side it assumed a gloomy, awe-inspiring character, while on the other side it wore a joyous aspect, inviting to mirth and pleasure. The second system rested on a total separation of God from nature, and thus it acquired a monotonous, one-sided character of abstruseness, without any feeling for form and beauty: it was the system of the Egyptian priests and of the Israelites, and in after times passed over into Mohammedanism and some Christian sects as Unitarianism, etc. The third system also postulated the separation of God and nature, but it was not a definitive separation, for there was hope of a reconciliation; it consisted, therefore, in a sense of alienation from God, and in an incessant longing for reunion with him. This system found embodiment in the Grecian mysteries and the Pythagoreo-Orphic societies, and later in "positive" Christianity: it was neither absolutely polytheistic nor absolutely monotheistic, but compact of these two systems, in that it contemplated many gods embraced under one form, or one god manifested in sundry forms. Even in the myths underlying the Eleusinian mysteries we have a conversion of the gods, especially Demeter and Dionysos, into human form and a resurrection and ascension of Persephone; an important part was played in the same mysteries by the bread and wine employed for religious purposes, by the purifications in water, and by the fasts observed; in the Bacchic mysteries Orpheus, Zagreus, and others appear as suffering and dying demigods; in the Orphic rites there is allusion to the natural sinfulness of man, and to grace and redemption; in the mysteries of Cybele sexual continence is commended as highly meritorious; in the mysteries and in the Pythagorean sect, even as in Christianity, the bodily life is regarded as an evil, an incorporeal immortality of the soul as true bliss, stress is laid on the soul's delights, and on the punishment of the wicked, whereas, in polytheism the soul after death is but a shadow; and many are the other points of contact between those systems and Christianism, which, being of a more general nature, have not yet been mentioned in these pages, for example certain mysterious and enigmatical personages who have remained hitherto quite unnoticed, except by the learned.

Commonly schools and the books give information only about the officially recognized Olympian gods, and perhaps the gods of sea and netherworld; but the "Best God," in Greek Aristaios, is passed over in silence, just because one knows not what to make of him.

This Aristaios passed for a son of Apollo the god of light. Held apart from the "scandalous chronicles" and naughty gossip that was in circulation around the rest of the gods, he was represented as inventor of sheep-husbandry, beekeeping, the production of oil from the olive, etc., as man's helper in drought and aridity, practicer of leechcraft (like his brother Aesculapius), subduer of the winds, originator of rites, laws, and sciences. As the little vogue of his name would indicate, he was less honored on the Grecian terra firma than in the Hellenic islands and colonies, and there ofttimes was joined with the father of the gods, as Zeus-Aristaios (particularly in his role of protector of the bees), with the god of light as Aristaios-Apollon, with the god of fertility as Aristaios-Dionysos. In the island Ceos he was the most highly reverenced of all the gods. Thus we see in Aristaios a conception of cne almighty, allwise god, transcending all the conceptions of polytheism, and all the gods in human form worshiped by ancient Greece.

Now plainly Aristeas and Aristaios are one same name. Among the ancient Greeks there was a mythical personage named Aristeas. He was Apollo's priest, as his paronymus was Apollo's son. According to Herodotus (IV. 13-15) Aristeas was of Proconnesus, an isle in the Propontis (sea of Marmora), son of Castrpbius; in the sacred trance received the inspiration of Apollo, journeyed into Scythia (north of the Black Sea), and died in his native place, in a fulling-mill. The place having been closed after his death, a citizen of the neighboring town of Cyzicus who happened to be passing, declared that he had just before met Aristeas in that town and spoken with him. The mill door was then opened, but no trace of Aristeas was there. Seven years afterward he appeared again in Proconnesus, there composed poems on his journey to Scythia (which Herodotus read), and disappeared a second time. But 340 years later he was seen at Metapontum, in lower Italy, where he ordered the citizens to erect to Apollo a statue with his name; then he disappeared for good. On questioning the oracle at Delphi what they should do, the burghers of Metapontum were counseled to obey the precept of Aristeas; which they did. Herodotus saw the statue surrounded by laurel trees. This "Best of Men," ever reappearing, and anon disappearing, without leaving any vestige of bodily presence, is no doubt evidence of a pre-Christian need of a son of god rising from the dead and ascending into heaven; as far as it goes, it is also an argument for the reality of resurrection from the dead and for the union of the divine and human.

But not only occurrences which call to mind the Christian Son of God, but even his very name appears in Grecian antiquity; and indeed the name antedates the occurrences. Homer (Odyssey, V. 125), and Hesiod (Theogony 969) mention Jasion or Jasios (names closely resembling the Hebrew Joshua and Jesus), a son of Zeus, who had a sister Harmonia, and who with the goddess Demeter (the earth, or fertility) produced out of a thrice plowed field Plutus (wealth): meaning that the discoverer of husbandry became discoverer of thrift. But in punishment of his sacrilegious love of a goddess Zeus struck him dead with a thunderbolt, yet at the same time assigned him a place among the gods. As beloved of the Eleusinian goddess, Jasios, after initiation into the mysteries by Zeus himself, became the indefatigable herald of the mystic doctrines. Says Diodorus (V. 49): "Wealth is a gift imparted through the intermediation of Jasios...

It is known of all that these gods (Demeter, Jasios, and Plutos), when invoked amid dangers by the initiated straightway offered them help; and whoso hath part in the mysteries, the same will be more devout, more upright, and in every respect better." Thus does Jasion figure as son of the highest god, as himself raised to divine honors, as a wandering apostle of religion, and as the source of all good fortune. His name is equivalent to "savior," "healer," being from the same root as iatros (healer), and the verb iaomai (to heal, cure). Compare Iao, the Greek form of the Hebrew divine name Yahve or Jehova; also* Iacchos, and Jason (i. e., Iason).

Thus in mystic Hellenism we find the basic ideas of the later system of divine incarnation and human deification, of redemption, etc.; and there can be no doubt that we must seek in the Grecian mysteries for one of the sources of Christianism.

PART FOURTH
Son of Man. Son of God

1. Hellenism and Judaism

IF ONE ATTENDS solely to the fact that the founder of th!e Christian religion was a Jew, and that not only he executed his mission in Judea, but took Judaism for the basis of his teaching, the assertion made in the preceding section, viz.: that the sources of Christianism are to be sought in the Grecian mysteries, may appear singular. But the apparent contradiction disappears at once when we reflect that long before Christ's day Judaism was thoroughly yeasted with Grecian elements; and that after his death the work of propagating his system was done far more largely by Greeks and men of Grecian education than by Jews. We will not only prove that this was so, but also will show that the Christianism of Christians is at root and in substance a totally different thing from the Christianism of Jesus.

Sharper contrast can hardly be than that between the Grecian and the Jewish character. On one side closest union between God and world: on the other, widest divulsion; on one side most untiring research and the finest sense of art-form: on the other only theology and religious poetry; on the one side a priesthood that makes no pretension, and has little or no influence: on the other a nation ruled by priests; the Greeks maintaining an active commerce with all the world, their ships traversing the seas, from the Strait of Gibraltar to the remotest angle of the Etixine: Judea sealed against all access from without, against every ship that touched at Joppa, against every caravan from the desert; in Greece eager seizing of everything new and readiness to reject what is antiquated: in Judea holding fast to what is old and mistrust of all change.

These fundamentally different elements were fated to come in mutual contact. Ever since their liberation from Babylonian captivity by the decree of Cyrus, the Jews, both those who remained in the region of Euphrates and Tigris and the small number of them who returned to the native land, had lived under the Persian sceptre, and therefore after the conquest of Persia by Alexander, were exposed to the powerful influence of Grecian culture. The Jews were scattered still more in consequence of the wars between Alexander's successors: soon they were to be found in every port and every isle of the Mediterranean as far as Spain; on the edge of the Asian and African deserts; and after this dispersion (in Greek, diaspora), they became a shop keeping or mercantile race. But nowhere outside Palestine were they so numerous as in Egypt and its splendid new capital, Alexandria, seat of Grecian art, literature and learning. They enjoyed large privileges in Egypt; and they erected at Leontopolis a temple, after the model of the temple at Jerusalem. But though the Jews of the Diaspora, thanks to their laws regarding foods and the Sabbath, their possession of the Scriptures, their undiminished reverence for the Temple of Jerusalem, and the obligation laid on every Jew to pilgrim thither once at least, remained most firmly attached to the religion of their fathers, nevertheless in many places they adopted the language (usually Greek) of the locality in which they lived, so that a special "Hellenist" synagogue had to be erected at Jerusalem for the sake of visiting Jews who understood only Greek. But nowhere did Jews adopt the Grecian customs and language so unreservedly as at Alexandria, and it was there that between the years B.C. 280 and 220 the Pentateuch was translated into Greek. This translation still is styled the Septuagint (Latin, Septuaginta, Greek, Heptekonta, both meaning seventy), in accordance with the old fable that in the work were employed seventy-two translators, being six from each of the twelve Israelitish tribes; and that while each of the seventy-two translated the whole of the five "books of Moses," the several versions agreed verbatim, literatim, punctatim. In later times the remainder of the Hebrew Bible was translated (about 125 B.C.).

In Alexandria scholars who were not Jews found in the Septuagint an introduction to Jewish theology; the Hellenist Jews, from their acquaintance with the literature of Greece, became conversant with Grecian philosophy. Greeks began to admire the wisdom of Moses, Jews to study Plato and Aristotle; and the enlightened polytheism of the one concurred with the monotheism of the others, in developing a new mysticism. In this mysticism of the Alexandrines it was that the idea of Divine Revelation had its origin an idea before unknown, but now suddenly taken up by these enthusiasts, and applied, on the one side to the Old Testament, and on the other side to the Greek philosophers. The Jew Aristobulus, founder of this school of thought, by means of an allegorical interpretation of the

Old Testament, traced to that source all the wisdom of the Greeks; and Philo, greatest of the Jewish philosophers, contemporary with Jesus, though he knew nothing of his life or doctrine, so spiritualized the tradition of his race as to see in the four rivers of Eden the four cardinal virtues, in the trees of Paradise the other virtues, in the patriarchs and heroes of Israel only personifications of various moral conceptions: all in the Grecian manner. According to Philo, before he created the world, God made a world of ideas, which found its centre of unity in his Word (logos); the corporeal world was made after the model of this ideal world. The logos was God's first work, the world his second: this passed afterward into the gospel called of John: "In the beginning was the word,!' etc. He understood the history of man's creation to mean that the first human creature was immortal, ideal, perfect, but that by the creation of woman he was made sinful, imperfect. Philo took the idea of immortality from the Grecian philosophy rather than from the ancient Jewish doctrines; and with Pythagoras he regards the soul's union with the body as a punishment. He therefore taught that man should free himself as much as possible from this burdensome association, that is, should despise sense and live entirely in the thought of God, that so he might obtain release. One should think such views are inconsistent with the laws of man's nature, and so in truth they are; but nevertheless in Philo's day there existed a society that aimed to fashion their life in accordance with these opinions.

2. The Essenes

SUCH A SOCIETY was the order or sect of the Essenes, who traced their origin back to high antiquity, but whose doctrines really were first put forth about the year 100 B.C. The Grecizing Jew Josephus makes them a "third party," standing between the Pharisees and the Sadducees. But the Essenes, as such, had nothing to do with the political questions at issue between the two principal parties. The Essenes constituted a secret society. The name, Essenes, Essenii, is of unknown derivation. But as they practiced the healing art they got the name of Thenapeutae (healers, physicians). Josephus says that they lived in special settlements in the country parts; Philo, that they lived in the hamlets, avoiding the cities; Pliny the elder plants them on the western shore of the Dead Sea, in settlements apart. Their number is stated at 4,000. Their occupations were husbandry and handicraft, but they sternly refused to have anything to do with whatever served the uses of warfare, as the manufacture of arms; they also declined all trades engaged in for individual profit, as traffic, seafaring, innkeeping. They had no private property, but community of goods; among themselves they neither bought nor sold, but each to each gave according to the need. They repudiated not alone servitude, but mastery in general, and whatever in anywise annuls the natural equality of mankind. Their food was such as necessity required, and was prepared strictly according to the rules of the order. On this point we know with certainty only that they held oil in abomination, whether for anointing or for use with victuals. But from the circumstance that they condemned bloody offerings and always practiced great abstemiousness in food, we must infer that they abstained totally from fleshmeat and intoxicating liquors. Sexual love also they condemned, and a party among them (the leading party), abstained from marriage and maintained its numerical strength by adopting outside children; another faction, however, deeming this strictness to be fatal to the sect, retained the in stitution of marriage, though under severe restrictions. The members observed the most scrupulous cleanliness, taking the bath daily in cold water, and wearing white garments. , Their daily tasks were minutely prescribed. Before rise of sun they spoke no word, only the prayers, in which they paid honor to the sun as symbol of God. Then they went about their work, coming thence back to the common meal, first washing themselves and putting on clean garments. No one tasted anything till the priest had made prayer. The meal concluded, they offered prayer in unison, laid off their clean garments, and went back to work. At the last meal of the day the same customs were observed: at meat only one person spoke at a time. They did nothing without orders from the superiors, practiced moderation in all things, studied to control the passions, to be faithful to all obligations, to be at peace among themselves and with all the world, and to be helpful to the poor. There was a twelve-month term of probation prior to admission into the order. During that time the postulant conformed to the Essenian rule of life: he received a small hatchet (borne by all Essenes, as an emblem of labor), a loincloth for the bath, and a white gown. If the result of probation was satisfactory, a second term of probation (two years) followed;

if found worthy, the postulant was admitted to membership. The rite of admission consisted of a meal in common, preceded by the pronouncing of the vow by the new brother. The tenor of the vow was that he obligated himself to be ever faithful to the rules of the order and to lead a virtuous life; to observe secrecy regarding" the doings of the order and the names of members: this with reference to the world without; but with regard to the society itself, to keep nothing secret from the brethren. After admission, the Essenes were classed in four degrees. Unworthy members were expelled a terrible punishment, indeed, for the outcasts were not released from their vow, and yet could not in the world comply with it; and so were doomed to perish.

Their religious views have been already stated in part. With Judaism their only bond of union was in their practice of sending to the temple at Jerusalem offerings; but by reason of their condemnation of bloody sacrifices they were self-excluded from the temple. Nor was their belief in immortality of Jewish origin, for they held that soul, formed of most tenuous aether, is attracted and appropriated by a body, within which it lives as a prisoner; but that after liberation through death it soars to heaven, where it lives for evermore in a blest land, without rain, or snow, or heat, while the wicked are tortured in a remote region of cold and darkness. This recalls the views of the Pythagoreans. Less honorable to the Essenes are 'the frauds practiced by many of them in pretending to read the future, to interpret dreams, to conjure disease away, etc. Of later Christian notions we are reminded by the Essenian nomenclature of the angels, and the obligation imposed on new members to keep the names secret. The Essenian order survived till the early days of Christianism: it then died out, the Christian asceticism having made it superfluous.

3. Christianism

ESSENISM IS ONE of those phenomena which make but a small figure in general history, but which have mighty results, and which reconcile contrarieties in human nature. For in Essenism we have the middle term between the Grecian mysteries and Christianism, as also between the Grecian philosophy and Judaism. As appears from what has gone before, the Essenian society was a Judaic imitation of the Pythagorean league, and that league, again, represented in philosophy what the Grecian mysteries represented in religion, namely, humiliation of man by showing him that there exist higher powers that far transcend humanity; and then the elevation of man by inculcation of the thought of immortality and of future union with the Creator. With {his mysticism was associated, in Greece, the lofty morality of a Socrates, a Plato, an Aristotle; and in Judea the belief in One God. The combination of all these elements could have but one result, to wit, to call forth that great power which transformed the world Christianism.

This now power was bound to arise, to reconcile contraries that confronted each other in that time, after the Roman Empire had brought under its universal sway the lands that had cradled all the diverse religions and philosophies. Those religious and philosophical systems were no longer, as before, separated: brisk inter-communication favored by the commerce and the wars of the vast empire, brought them daily into contact. The result was twofold: first, a certain indifference for religious opinions, the diversity of which gave men occasion to judge that in supersensual things no direct knowledge is possible; and the mischief of it all was that nothing was done for the education or enlightenment of the people, and, in fact, science existed only for the higher orders, and the people found no substitute for their ancient belief. But secondly, the result also was that people began to be conscious of the feeling, implanted by the Grecian philosophers, and particularly by the Stoics, that in spite of national and religious differences, all men are brothers, and that mankind is one great whole. However beautiful and noble this idea, it had to lie dormant so long as no bond of spiritual kinship save that of political unity held together the peoples who within the empire jointly obeyed one law and one will. This missing bond of spiritual union could not be other than a religious one; for so long as the sciences were so undeveloped no other spiritual guidance but that Godward could lead all hearts, however educated, of whatever nation, to the one end toward which men were being forced by the consciousness that, above all, they were men. And if it be asked what sort of a religion that must be which shall satisfy all nations at once, first of all it is very clear that it could be no polytheistic religion. That form of religion had outlived its usefulness. The various national religions Egyptian, Chaldaean, Syrian, Grecian, Roman had completely exhausted themselves in the production of deities: polytheism could give forth no more new shoots, as was shown by the fact that the Romans, all the forces of nature having been worked up, had gone and made goddesses of the virtues, e. g., Pudicitia, Concordia, Pax, Victoria, and the rest, had no recourse but to admit to their Pantheon all the gods of the conquered nations, and paid now to Isis, Cybele, Mithras, and Baal the same worship as before they had paid to Jupiter and Juno. Into such disrepute had polytheism fallen in the estimation of all educated men, who if they were persons of serious character despised such gods; but if they were frivolous, ridiculed worship and sacrifice and oracles and priests. The priests themselves smiled when they met, and by their irregular lives and their superstitious practices forfeited all respect. At last every honest man must have been transported with indignation when the emperors in the paroxysms of their despotic frenzy had themselves worshiped as gods and a race of hounds in human form burned the incense of adulation before them.

Hence, the new religion for which mankind sought, to give true expression to the sentiment of a common humanity, could not be any of the heathen systems. Rather, by insisting on the oneness of Godhead, it had to make an end of polytheism, of godmaking, and of Olympian wantoning, and at the same time, of scorn and derision of the gods.

Thus, then, what was wanted was a god who should have vanquished all other gods, and he a god of definite outline and fixed character no nebulous, lackadaisical, inert deity such as the Grecian philosophers preached: no abstract "world-soul" signifying nothing to the uneducated people; but a god like unto man himself, and whom man should have "made after his own likeness"; one with human feelings, sentiments, and passions, with human wrath and human lovingness. And this god must stand for a doctrine of personal immortality to the end the precious Ego of every man might have infallible and trustworthy assurance that his title to a Mansion in the Skies will stand unchallengeable forever and forever. And again, this god must be no abstract entity, alleged to have existed somewhere, somewhen, but a personality associated with definite localities, and possessing: very definite traits. And so the problem was to find this one god, this doctrine of immortality, to find a personality that would be the middle term between the two.

Nowhere was a monotheism to be found save in Judaism, and there it was plain and open to view. We have already seen how the Jews were scattered all over the world. Their synagogues were everywhere, and (noteworthy fact) they had proselytes in every large city, especially in Rome. In this we see the first steps in the dissemination of monotheism: but it could not be propagated on the large scale by Jews. Few were the persons who took a liking to the strictness of the Mosaic religion, and the God of the Jews was too spiritual a being to be grasped; besides, very many turned away from Judaism because of the indefiniteness of the Jewish notions of immortality, or the strange rites and the peculiar usages of the Jewish people.

From Judaism, then, the idea of monotheism was the only feature that could be borrowed: what was demanded else was the mystic element; that is to say, men wanted a system of religious conceptions that would reflect back upon them their own sentiments as the infallible truth. But the material best fitted for that end was to be found in the mysteries and in the Pythagorean and Essenian doctrines. The diverse ideas of the several secret leagues with regard to the separation of the divine from the human and their reconciliation, must find their unity in the Jewish God a thing not difficult to accomplish in the times immediately preceding the advent of Christ, because of the intermingling of Grecian and Jewish ideas: and this unity had to be established by some personage of imposing figure on the stage of history, who should impress his seal upon it and surround it with the prestige of deity.

Now, at that time there was both among the heathen and the Jews an expectation of some such divine intervention as this. Thus, in the early years of the Roman Empire the belief was widespread that a new kingdom was to be founded in the East, and that a new Golden Age was about to begirt. More definite was the expectation entertained by the Jews of a Messiah to come, who would restore the kingdom of Israel, and the worship of Jehova. This longing of the Jews coincided with the desire of heathendom for a new religion to take the place of a dying and degenerate polytheism.

4. Jesus

AT THIS JUNCTURE appeared Jesus. He lived and died in obscurity. Of his career not one word of mention is found in contemporary Greek and Roman writers, eagerly as they investigated everything. But this obscurity wrought no detriment, for it left those who were longing for a new religion free to make of him whatever they thought best for their cause; that is to say, they made of him a personality very different from what he really was. Out of a circumcised son of a Jewish carpenter, who rose, indeed, above the bigotry of his people, and who suffered death for his revolt against the rule of priests and scribes, was developed the longed-for Messiah. He was no longer merely human, but the Son of God, born of a virgin; a thaumaturge; his death was formally and intentionally a sacrifice for the "redemption" of mankind; after death he rose again, and then ascended into heaven: in a word, Jesus the man had become a god. And thus on the Jewish branch were grafted quite unJewish, Graecomystical shoots till the branch was no longer recognizable.

We thus have in the life of the founder of the Christian Church, as handed down to us, two elements, truth and fiction. The element of truth is whatever is consistent with historical research and psychological fact and nature's laws; and the element of fiction comprises whatever is in conflict with these. Jesus himself never pretended to be more than a man. Virtue was the burden of his teaching, and he never propounded a creed. To the many names of God he added that of "Father" father of all mankind. He was no dogmatist, but a moral reformer, and as such occupied' common ground with the Essenes and with John the Baptist, though he differed from them, and particularly from the Essenes, with regard to methods and measures: the Essenes would save men's souls by withdrawing them from human society; Jesus sought to save men living in the world to save human society itself.

Jesus taught the people in parables, enforcing his doctrine of virtuous living by the use of similes that no hearer could fail to understand. Those who afterward essayed to write the history of his life and work, in like manner made a free use of figurative language, and the personality of Jesus was glorified, and his "mission" magnified till the world saw in him, indeed, "the desired of all the nations," the Messiah longed for by Israel, the reconciler of the divine and the human, toward whom all the mysteries had pointed.

The miracles of Jesus, namely, acts and occurrences that contradict the laws of nature, are not actual events; for as they are recorded in the New Testament they show a needless abrogation of natural law needless, because the truths which Jesus preached could not be made more true by miracles. And thus, as the rationalists of the 18th century explained them as actual occurrences indeed, but yet as in accordance with the natural law, so now they are held to be quite needless juggleries altogether unworthy of Jesus. Hence the rational interpretation of the miracles is, that they represent the effort of the evangelists to portray the life and person of the Master in such colors as their notions of his supereminent dignity required. We divide these miracles into three classes the miracles of the birth, the life, and the death of Jesus.

The birth, of Jesus, as narrated in the gospel story, is itself a miracle. The legitimate son of Joseph, the carpenter of Nazareth, and of Mary for such he was, according to the genealogy found in Matthew and Luke had to be transformed into the Son of God, nay, made God himself, if his doctrine was to appear as of divine origin. Of types of such transformation there was no lack in heathendom. The first Christians, it is true, knew nothing of the sun-god Buddha, born again of a woman, but they were acquainted with Grecian and Roman mythology. Apollo, himself a god, walked on earth as a shepherd. Herakles, son of Zeus, and Romulus, son of Mars and of a virgin, were founders of states and cities, and progenitors of nations; then why should not the founder of a religion and of a church be also son of God and of a virgin? Nay, why might not God himself walk on earth in human form? That such was the actual origin of the story of the Divine Birth is not doubtful: all the rest is mere embellishment as when the angel announces to the virgin the coming birth of the Son of God; when another angel, accompanied by the heavenly hosts, tells the shepherds of his actual birth; when a star conducts the "wise men of the East" to the wondrous babe, and they, with the shepherds and Simeon and Anna, pay him homage; and when Herod, purposing to take the life of the predestined Messiah, in order to compass that end orders the slaughter of the innocents.

The miracles of the life of Jesus are either abrogations of natural laws, or cures of diseases, or resuscitations from the dead, or apparitions. All these different kinds of miracles are fictions with a purpose. We have already seen how in the Grecian mysteries bread and wine were employed as consecrated viands for the gods, and how at Eleusis divine honors were paid to Demeter and Dionysos as givers of bread and wine. Jesus, too, had to be made lord and giver of these two sacred viands: hence the change of water into wine, and the multiplication of the loaves; and later, in the last supper, bread and wine were made the object of the Christian Mysteries. The walking on the waters of the lake of Gennesareth, the stilling of the winds, the blasting of the fig tree, the finding of the penny in the fish's mouth, and Peters draught of fishes are pictures of the imagination designed to show the power of the Son of God over the waters, the air, the world of plants and of animals. So, too, his power over bodily diseases is made something real for the common understanding by such stories as the healing of paralytics, lepers, the blind, the deaf and dumb; over mental diseases by the freeing of the possessed, over death itself by the raising of the dead: Among the apparitions we reckon those of the Holy Spirit as a dove at the baptism of Jesus, of Satan at Jesus' temptation, and of Moses and Elias at the transfiguration: this is all allegory. The "Holy Spirit" is an idea distinct from God only in thought; the dove is the symbol of purity and gentleness. The Devil is a personification of evil, and the failure of his attempt was the triumph of the good. As for the transfiguration, that typifies the vast superiority of the new law over the old: the old must do homage to the new.

The miracles of Jesus' death, viz., the darkening of the sun, the rending of the veil of the Holy of Holies in the Temple, the resurrection of the dead, were occurrences quite inomissible at the death of a god; they betoken the mourning of nature and of religion. But the miracles that followed his death, the resurrection and the ascension, together with the apparitions of the Crucified in the mean time, were imagined purely and plainly to confirm the belief in an everlasting redeemer and in the personal immortality of each individual one of the faithful.

Of far greater importance than the miracles of Jesus are his teachings, and in particular his fine discourse on the mountain, also his beautiful parables. But his utterances contain nothing that is essentially new, the same thoughts having been often expressed by religious teachers and sages of other times and in other lands; and yet they possess a charm all their own, by reason of their unassuming simplicity. It was not the doctrine of the unity of God and of love for the neighbor that wrought the propagation of his teachings the Jews possessed that doctrine already; nor was it his call to a higher life than that of sense the Grecian philosophers preceded him in that respect; nor his alleged divinity, nor the miracles ascribed to him his contemporaries in every land had had experience of miracles in every shape: it was the forcefulness, the grandeur, the simplicity of his discourse, speaking to the heart of man and mastering it, and calming its unrest. Here he was self-based and individual, supreme and irresistible. His teaching, and in particular the sermon on the mount, is the most emphatic, blistering condemnation of those who, for the last nineteen hundred years, have called themselves not only Christians, but the only Christians; who, nevertheless, in open contempt of their supposed Master, not only take oaths, and require an eye for an eye, cherish mortal hate for their enemies, trumpet their almsgiving abroad, offer their prayers aloud at the street crossings, fast ostentatiously, lay up for themselves treasures on earth, which are eaten by the moth and the rust; serve two masters or more, see the mote, though blind to the beam, throw the holy thing to the dogs, when one asks them for a loaf give him a stone, do not unto others as they would that others should do unto them: who not only do all this, but who even enact laws which oblige men to do all this. He whom they hypocritically call Master, but whom they never have understood, were he to appear among them, would anathematize them in the noble words, I know you not. Depart from me, ye doers of evil ! Such language was unheard before his day; therefore wondered the people, for he spake with power, and not like the scribes and pharisees.

5. The Early Christians

WHAT THEN, IS the difference between the Christianism of Jesus and the Christianism of Christians? The former, as seen in the discourses of the New Testament, and above all in the ever beautiful sermon on the mount, is a simple and unpretending, yet world-transforming doctrine of God, Virtue, and Love of Man: a monotheism borrowed from the Jews for the behoof of all men, but purified of ceremonialism, sabbatism, sacrifices, highpriesthood: in short, the Christianism of Jesus meant the coming "Kingdom of God," in which the virtuous man would enjoy happiness and peace. But the Christianism of Christians is a Mysticism ingrafted on this monotheism, comprising the dogmas of the Incarnation, Atonement, Redemption, Resurrection, and Second Coming, and the Miracles invented to buttress these dogmas. The Christianism of Jesus fell when he and his first disciples died: they had no hair-splitting theology, only a devout heart: that system was too simple, too unadorned, too little flattering to sense and to man's vainglory to cut any figure in the world. But the Christianism of Christians, which had for its mother the Grecian mysteries, borrowed from Jesus, its father (without whose personality and name it never could have lived at all), what little was known concerning him, but swadded it in a thick wrappage of mystic dogmatism. Let us see how this dogmatic Christianism succeeded in erecting itself upon the simple ethic-religious system of Jesus, and in making itself a power in the world by evolving new mysteries. Were it not for the grafting on it of the Graeco-mystical elements, Christianism would never have grown to be even a church, to say nothing of its prospects of becoming a power in the world. Its adherents in the beginning were good, zealous, believing folk, but among them were no men of education or of commanding ability. The first congregation in Jerusalem, therefore, unable to comprehend the lofty views of the Crucified, took their stand on a narrow ground not essentially different from that of Judaism; for example, they held that no one was worthy to be baptized who would not first undergo circumcision, thus becoming by adoption a Jew. The Apostle James, a devout ascetic, was the head of this school, the adherents of which were called Jewish Christians. The first to demand repudiation of Judaism was Stephen, a man of Grecian education; but he paid the penalty of his ambitious plans by a martyr's death. The congregation at Antioch adopted Stephen's view, according to which the "Gentile Christians" and the "Jewish Christians" stood on an equality. The intellectual leader of the Gentile-Christian school was Paul, a man who, in talents and in force of character, stood high above all the original apostles of the Nazarene. Through Paul's exertions Christianism overstepped the narrow limits of Palestine and Syria. Well schooled, both in Grecian philosophy and Jewish theology, he was at the first a fanatical persecutor of the Christians, but had a sudden conversion while journeying to Damascus on a persecuting raid, and thenceforth was a zealous apostle of the new religion. Being a victim of epilepsy, Paul had frequent fits and visions, and he spoke of them often, thus implanting in the minds of the Christians a firm belief in such occurrences. Of course, the way was thus made ready for the introduction of the legends of a resurrection, an ascension, etc. Furthermore, a foundation was in this way laid for a great theological superstructure, which very soon was seen to rise. As the foundation, so was the superstructure mystical. Over against the first man, Adam, representing the sensuous life, sin, servitude, and death, Paul set up the God-man Christ, representing the spirit, grace, freedom, and life; man was to crucify the "old Adam," and to be born anew in Christ, even to become one with him. By this union, he said, the law of Moses is done, away, being superseded by faith whereby alone 'the sinner is justified and made worthy of God's grace. For true faith, he added, carries with it good works, and the true believer cannot be otherwise than righteous.

Paul thus stood, in a certain sense, on the Protestant ground as contradistinguished from the Judaeo-Christian (which is partly also the Catholic) ground of Peter, James, and John, who upheld the Mosaic law, and received into the Church only circumcised! converts. Peter wavered, being a Jew among Jews, but often forgetting the Mosaic law in the company of Gentile Christians; but Paul would never consent that Gentile converts should be obliged to conform to the Jewish rites: hence Paul was the real founder of the Christian Church, which, had his opponents been, victorious, would have remained a Jewish sect. The Church was split into two parties. To the Jewish-Christian party adhered the numerous converts from Essenism, with whom the tie of blood was stronger than the spiritual bond which united them with the school of Pythagoras. This party did not regard Jesus as God, but classed him with the angels.

Between the two parties, Judaeo-Christian and Gentile-Christian, arose a third party, that of the Alexandrine Christian Jews. Their leader was Apollos (properly Apollonius), of whom it is related in the Acts of the Apostles, that he recognized only the baptism of John, and not that of Jesus, but that he was converted to belief in the lattter by certain of Paul's disciples at Ephesus. He it was that imported into Christianism the Alexandrine doctrine of the Logos or Word.

6. The New Testament

WITH SUCH A distribution of parties, the New Testament literature arose. It may now be affirmed without hesitation that not one piece of this literature was composed by any of the disciples of Jesus, who were all uneducated men. The early Christians had, at first no Sacred Scripture other than the Old Testament; with regard to the doctrine of Jesus they depended on oral instruction. Even the language in which the New Testament was written, the Hellenistic (or literary dialect of the Alexandrines) is proof that it was the work of men of Greek education. As far as can be determined now the earliest New Testament writer was Paul. The Pauline epistles that are his indisputably, are those to the Romans, the Corinthians, and the Galatians; the most dubious among them are the epistles to Timothy, Titus, and Philemon. There are epistles of some of the other apostles, as James, Peter, John, and Jude, and these, of course, according to the party stand of their writers, represent views opposed to those of Paul. They are of later date than Paul's epistles, and are hardly to be credited to the apostles whose names are prefixed to them. To the Alexandrine school is to be referred the epistle to the Hebrews, distinguished from the Pauline writings by the fact that it holds the Old and New Testaments to be, not opposites, but complements of each other.

Apart from the Epistles the Revelation of John (Apocalypse) is the oldest book of the New Testament. Written in the spirit of an Old Testament prophet, it expresses the indignation of a Jew against the Romans during the siege and shortly before the destruction of Jerusalem, A. D. 70; it contains the prediction that not Jerusalem, but the whore of Babylon (Rome), together with the entire heathen world, will perish amid fire, blood, and ruin; but that there will be let down from Heaven a new and glorious Jerusalem, abode of the blest, seat of the "bride of the lamb." After the destruction of Jeru-salem the Apocalypse was written anew by an unknown hand, in the Christian sense. As everyone knows, the prophecies of the book did not come true; but its fantastic, morbid imaginings have ever since been interpreted by enthusiasts as infallible forewarnings of things to come; and many a searcher of its pages has lost what modicum of sense they ever had in working out its meaning.

The other historical writings of the New Testament consist of four Gospels and the Acts of the Apostles. It is now evident that, when in the course of time the oral traditions were committed to writing, Jesus' discourses, which, with an admirable simplicity and admirable clearness, 'expressed a good deal in a few words, must have been handed down in: far more authentic form than the history of his deeds; and that among his discourses, those which contained truths of general application were more faithfully remembered than those which expressed personal views as, for example, those in which he claims to be Messiah. The oldest written accounts of his life and work are lost to us forever; they were, without doubt, written in the language which was used by Jesus and his disciples, Aramaic, a sister tongue of Hebrew. Of the existing Gospels, written in Greek, the first three, called "synoptics" (i. e., agreeing), are based on one older original gospel or account; the third Gospel, John's, stands by itself. The new criticism regards Mark's Gospel as the most ancient: it contains almost exclusively narratives of facts, written down from memory, with the accruing embellishments and modifications; but Mark gives little of the discourses of Jesus; he says nothing, knows nothing of any supernatural birth of Jesus, and regards him simply as man. Mark's Gospel is the basis of the other two synoptics, which draw on him for narrative, while they both add the discourses. The Gospel according to Matthew gives the discourses a Judaeo-Christian tinge; that according to Luke (who also wrote the Acts) a Gentile-Christian coloring: but they both waver between the opinions that Jesus is God and man, and that he is only man. But the Gospel literature was lifted out of this state of hesitation by the fourth Gospel. This Gospel bears the name of the Judaeo-Christian apostle John, but erroneously, for it had its origin in the Alexandrine school, and was written probably A. D. 160 to 170. The Alexandrines, as we have seen, were wont to resolve all accounts of facts, whether real or fictitious, into mental concepts, and, therefore, lived in a cloudworld of ideas. Whereas, the first apostles regarded the Nazarene merely as man, and while for Paul and the evangelists Matthew and Luke he was a god-man, the Joannine Gospel makes him God, and represents his existence on earth in palpable human form, as a mere passing incident. Hence it proclaims him the "Word" (logos), which Philo Judaeus discovered; which Logos not only was "in the beginning" with God, but was God himself. For the author of the fourth Gospel the narrative of occurrences in the life of Jesus is a secondary matter, serving only as a setting for his own peculiar doctrines. Thus the doctrine of the godhead of Jesus is the result of Grecian influence. Besides these four generally received Gospels several others, in one place or another, at one time or another, have passed for revealed writings. They are written, some in Aramaic, some in Greek, some in Latin, and, since their uncanonical character was decided, have been classed as Apocrypha. Their contents, barring a few passages that show some elevation of thought, are mostly in the jejune and tasteless vein of those trivial accounts of miracles which we find in the canonical Gospels, such as the changing of water into wine, the cursing of the figtree, Peter's draught of fishes, etc.; or they are of a still more paltry sort, and tell of a number of miracles wrought by

Jesus in his childhood. There are also apocryphal Acts of Apostles, apocryphal Apocalypses, and apocryphal Epistles, all of them what we should now call "pamphlets" composed in the interest of parties in the church.

But the "Word" of the Joannine Gospel became the password for the reunion of all parties. The influences that had brought thousands of Gentiles into the Church were all too strong for the resistance of the Judaeo-Christian party to overcome. The little Judaeo-Christian fold had no choice, therefore, but either to go back to Judaism or to become Gentile Christians unless, they were ready to suffer excommunication by the latter. Only small fractions of the Jewish-Christian body held out as sects apart, while the union of the ever-multiplying Gentile Christians, now styled the "Catholic" church, unchurched the "heretics," and set up the "new law" in opposition to the old, as its own inviolable foundation. Thus came into being the present collection of New Testament books, the "Church Catholic" having, about the end of the second century, separated the apocryphal from the canonical Scriptures. But still for a long time the character of individual books was in dispute, and John's "Revelation," together with several of the Epistles, was till recent times regarded by different persons or parties as apocryphal. To the decrees of councils and popes alone is it owing that there exists today a canonical collection of Scriptures, and that the books of the Canon are held to be inspired.

7. The Elements of the Church

IN THIS WISE was Christianism developed out of the secret associations of the ancient world. The early Christians themselves were, while under persecution, in a certain sense ai secret society. Their worship possessed an essentially mystic character. It was not so from the beginning. In Jesus' teachings there is not one word about divine service or cults; his surviving disciples knew of no other cult than the Jewish, and they assembled for "breaking bread" in their houses without any parade. Not until the Christians had been excluded from the synagogues were distinctive rites developed among them. There arose among them prophets whose inspired words were the principal feature of the religious service. Psalms were sung, not yet in the grand, impressive melodies of the Middle Age, but in "the long-drawn, partly nasal moaning tones, still usual in Eastern lands tones that defy all musical harmony." Besides, men then "spake tongues," or at least uttered "heaven-storming words" pell-mell in the heat of enthusiasm, which no one, speaker or hearer, could well understand; and men "prophesied," especially about the end of the world, the too slow oncoming of which caused much wonderment in those days. All these stupidities, by degrees, gave way before the efforts of strong-willed men like Paul. The "words in meeting" and the Lord's Supper (or Love Feast), fell into the background, and the supper came to be simply a souvenir of the Saviour's death, and at last was developed into a sacrament possessing the character of a "mystery;" i. e., a performance that must remain inscrutable to men, though it was men that contrived it. Baptism was associated as a sacrament with the supper, and the mysteries were multiplied. We have already seen how the mysteries of the Incarnation and Resurrection arose, namely, out of the necessity of giving to Jesus the stamp of deity, for without that Christianism never would have attained a commanding place ini the world. How to these mysteries, by the purely human decrees of the Nicaean Synod, the supreme and most incomprehensible mystery of all was added, the mystery of the Trinity; how, because of the impossibility of coming to agreement regarding this, the Church Catholic was split into the Roman and Greek, or Western and Eastern churches; how in the Western Church the bishops of Rome achieved supremacy; all this belongs, not to the history of the mysteries, but to the history of the Church.

PART FIFTH

A Pseudo-Messiah. A Lying Prophet

1. Apollonius of Tyana

GREAT MUST HAVE been the amazement of the Greeks when of a sudden, in different localities within the broad Roman Empire, communities arose which announced the suffering and dying God Jasios as the savior of a new age a Jasios who, under the form of a Jew, all unknown outside his own country, had but lately been crucified; whereas, Jasios, as all Initiates of the Eleusinia and of the mysteries of Samothrace well knew, was ages and ages before slain by the thunderbolt of Zeus. And still populations were passing day after day over to the crucified Jew, the Son of God, the wonderworker, who rose from the grave, who went up to heaven. And, in consequence of his teaching, though, after all, that did but complement the teaching of a Pythagoras, a Socrates, a Plato, the noble statues of the Grecian gods were falling from their bases. Ought the Beautiful to fall in order to make room for the Good? Might not both stand side by side? And if a son of God and a thamaturge was required, might not one be found without making of Zeus the Thunderer a victim to that fearful Jewish Yahve of Mt. Sinai?

And such a son of God and wonderworker they found. The

heathen prophet Apollonius of Tyana was a contemporary of Jesus, and was deeply venerated. And, as it chanced, a certain learned Greek, Flavius Philostratus, wrote 'a heathen gospel of the life of this Grecian saint, not as one hostile toward the Christians, nor as one who would prove their doctrine false, but with intent to come to the aid of decaying heathendom, and prevent for a time its over-throw by Christianism. To attain this end there must be no mention of Christianism or its author, so that Olympus might tower again in all its ancient glory and triumph over Sinai and Tabor. Philostratus composed his work, as he states, out of the notes of a disciple of Apollonius, one Damis, native of Ninive, by order of Julia Domna, wife of the Emperor Septimius Severus. What part of his work consisted of matter drawn from Damis's notes, and what he added out of his own fancy, we can never determine. But he showed true insight in making out his hero to have been a Pythagorean. He therefore rep-resents Apollonius as deriving his wisdom indirectly from the most ancient mysteries, those of Egypt, and from the venerated Grecian sacred leagues.

Apollonius was born in Tyana, a town in Cappadocia. Previous to his birth, says Philostratus, the god Proteus appeared to his moth-er and told her that the child soon to see the light was the God himself. This happened in:a meadow, where, after gathering flowers, she had fallen asleep, while swans gathered round her and intoned) their song. When the child was grown up he became a strict observ-er of the Pythagorean rule of life, abstaining from fleshmeat and wine, and wearing linen garments. His abode was a temple sacred to Aesculapius, god of healing. Unworthy offerers of gifts to the god he drove out, and healed such of the sick as repented of their trans-gressions. He rejected the Grecian mythology as fabulous, preferring far to it the fables of Esop, and his only prayer was addressed to the sun. He refused to take possession of an estate inherited from his father, and imposed on himself a silence of several years' duration. During his extensive travels he always lodged in temples, corrected abuses in the conduct of the divine service, couched his teachings in brief sentences, gathered around him disciples, of whom one was false and a, traitor; sided with the persecuted and righted the wrongs of the oppressed. Everywhere he understood the languages of the natives without learning them, and even read the thoughts of men; but the language of the beasts he learned from the Arabs of Meso-potamia. On entering that country the publican asked him whether he had with him anything subject to toll. The answer of Apollonius was that he carried about righteousness, temperance, a manly soul and a patient spirit and many another virtue named he. The sullen taxman, who had no mind for anything that lay outside his own duties, took the names of virtues for names of women, saying: "There, your maids are all down in the book." But Apollonius calmly went his way, with the brief remark: "They are not maids, but high-born dames;" nor paid he impost oni his ideal goods. In spite of his frankness of speech he was treated with great distinction by the king of that country. He told the king that he would best strengthen his royal power by honoring many and putting trust in but a few. The king, who was ill, having been comforted by the prophet, con-fessed that he had been freed from anxiety, not only with regard to his kingdom, but also with regard to death. From Babylon Apollonius bent his steps toward India, and there, according to the highly embellished story, saw men four or five ells in height, also men who were half white and half black; dragons, too, of various size he saw. He constantly carried on with Damis, the one disciple who accompanied him, instructive conversations) about the animals and the people whom they met. An Indian king, dazzled by the splendor of the prophet's genius, would not wear the crown in his presence. With the Brahmans, many of whose conjurfeats are recorded, e. g., flitting through the air, or at touch of their wands causing the earth to spring aloft, Apollonius swapped wisdoms; and as, in the opinion of Damis, the wisdom of the Brahmans was derived from Pythagoras, it was from Pythagoras also, of course, that they got their doctrine of metempsychosis. We learn that Apollonius also entertained that curious idea, and that he imagined himself to have been once an Indian taxgatherer, and was wont to tell of many incidents of that phase of his life. Furthermore, in his presence the Brahmans cured the possessed, the lame, the blind, and women in difficult labor, by imposition of hands, and by giving good counsels practices resembling those used in our day by sympathists, so-called. Apollonius returned to Babylon and Ninive, passing through fabulous lands, and then journeyed to the Ionians of Asia Minor. Apollonius banished from Ephesus an epidemic which was there raging, by requiring the citizens to stone a beggar in whom he discerned the daemon who was the cause of the disease; the culprit, under the storm of stones, was changed into a dog. Voyaging by sea to Greece, the Sage Apollonius imposed on his shipmates with the story that Achilles had appeared unto him five ells in height, and before his eyes had grown to twelve ells. At Athens, where he arrived during the Eleusinian mysteries, the priests refused to initiate him, because he was a conjurer; whereupon the Sage of Tyana told them that already he knew more about the mysteries than the priests. This alarmed them, and they wished to recall their refusal; but it was Apollonius's turn now to refuse them, so he deferred to another time his initiation, but in public discourses let his light shine before the Athenians. In Athens, too, there was a, youth possessed, who laughed and cried without cause. Apollonius having detected the true nature of the ailment, of which no one else had any suspicion, with stern looks and words of menace confronted the daemon, who thereupon fled away, and in token of his passage overturned a statue that no one had touched. But the youth, rubbing his eyes as though waking from sleep, was. seen to be cured. At Corinth the Sage detected in the bride of a comely youth a lamia or empusa; i. e., one of a class of spectral beings that used to haunt people, and under pretense of being in love with them, would eat the flesh off their bones. In the presence of Apollonius all her arts and all her imps disappeared, and the spectre was unmasked and confessed her evil intent. At the Olympian Games also this apostle of the Pythagorean philosophy preached. His following was increased by the accession of several members with their slaves; these he called his "congregation." With them he went to Rome, where the infamous Nero then reigned, who had prohibited philosophy, which he classed with soothsaying. But one who was in the service of the tyrant, impressed by the wisdom of the traveler, allowed him to lecture in the temples, and to these lectures there was great concourse. But one of his disciples who had accompanied him from Corinth, and who in Rome had ventured to condemn publicly the conduct of Nero and the prevailing immorality, was expelled the city by Tigellinus, captain of the emperor's bodyguard, and trusty tool of the tyrant, while Apollonius himself was kept under surveillance. But not only could nothing be proved against him; his wisdom filled even the sanguinary minions with admiration, though he spoke to them only the stern truth. For example, being asked by Tigellinus why he had no fear of Nero, he answered: "The God who makes him an object of fear made me fearless." Asked what he thought of Nero, "Better than you do," be replied; "ye think him gifted for singing, l for silence." Whereupon Tigellinus: "Go wherever youl please; you are stronger* than (any power 'of mine." A bridle in Rome having died, the body was on the way to the place of interment. Apollonius bade the bearersi to halt, touched the damsel, uttering some secret words, and called her back from death. Philostratus himself is in doubt whether the death was not apparent only. The philosopher then journeyed to the Strait of Gibraltar, whence he traversed Spain, Sicily and Greece, and then revisited Egypt. At Alexandria he recognized the innocence of one among eight criminals, interceded for him and had the man's execution put off till the last moment; then arrived the order to spare his life; he had confessed only under torture. The story is also told that Apollonius, on paying a visit to Vespasian, in Alexandria, "made him Caesar," thus giving to the Roman Empire once again, after a long interval, a just ruler; but after Vespasian's elevation to the throne, the philosopher frankly spoke the truth to him, when the Emperor annulled, as an unjust privilege, the liberties of Greece, which Nero had in a capricious humor granted on the occasion of the Olympian Games. Leaving Egypt, Apollonius journeyed to Ethiopia to visit the Gymnosophists, who dwelt in a sort of little republic of their own, on a mountain, and conducted a famous school. Probably because they were less conceited, went naked, and performed no magical feats, our Sage deemed them less wise than the Brahmans, and had resultless controversies with them about the relative superiority of Grecian and Egyptian art, the former representing the gods as resembling man, the latter as resembling animals. In that region Apollonius exorcised a satyr that was said to have killed two women. About the time of the taking of Jerusalem by Titus, Apollonius happened to be in the neighborhood of that city, and praised the Roman general for his "moderation" (though it was a curious sort of moderation which leveled a great city with the ground). Titus answered: "I have made conquest of Solyma; you have made conquest of me," and thereafter employed Apollonius as his adviser. At Tarsus he not only cured a young man of hydrophobia, but the dog also that had bitten him.

Having boldly denounced the Emperor Domitian at Ephesus, Apollonius was betrayed by his disciple Euphrates, and a plot was laid against him. Straightway he took ship for Rome, to confront the tyrant in his palace. In Rome he was thrown into prison, and treated with much harshness; but he defended himself with great spirit against the charges brought by his accuser, and was acquitted. Thereupon he uttered a tirade of reproaches against Domitian's satellites, and suddenly vanished miraculously from the judgment hall, appearing the same day in the vicinity of Naples, where he had friends. From Naples he went to Ephesus; there, in ecstasy, he saw the assassination of Domitian, at that moment taking place in Rome; then he died. None knew what age he had attained, whether 80 years or 100, nor the time, nor the place, nor the manner of his death. According to Philostratus he appeared after his death to a young man of his native town, Tyana, who doubted the immortality of the soul, and invoked Apollonius to explain the matter; but he was invisible to the other persons present.

2. Alexander, the False Prophet

IT IS NO matter of surprise that the cold, austere virtue and wisdom, the rather hollow religion, and the clumsy miracles of Apollonius neither built up a school for him nor kept the heathen religion on its feet; and though the emperors of the third century, from Caracalla to Diocletian, consecrated temples to him, and one of them, Alexander Severus, placed his bust, with those of Moses, Socrates and Jesus, in his private chapel, nevertheless the Sage of Tyana was soon forgotten, and with him, alas! the memory of his noble courage in the presence of tyrants. On the other hand, the charlatanry he practiced became more and more the order of the day, till at last it threw off all disguise. Whether this result is chargeable to his disciples, who, like the disciples of another master, prized his miracles more than his teachings, is a question that cannot be decided; but the fact is that soon after his death (the close of the first century) a number of impostors, wearing the cloak of religion, began to ply their trade. The satirist Lucian, who lived in the second century, and who made sport of everything religion and philosophy, gods and men, heathen and Christians has immortalized the tomfooleries of these pseudoprophets.

Of these the best known was Alexander of Abonotichus, in Asia Minor, a man greater in fraud, says Lucian, than his namesake, the son of Philip, in heroism. He was a large, handsome man, and by scrupulous care of his complexion, his hair, and his beard, enhanced the advantage nature had given him. But his character was "a compound of mendacity, fraud, perjury, and low tricks of every kind." In his boyhood he was apprenticed to a quack of Tyana, a renegade disciple of Apollonius (whose life, by the way, Lucian, who lived nearer to him than Philostratus, calls a "comedy"), and by him was instructed in all the artifices whereby one can outwit and defraud his fellows. After his master's death Alexander went into business on his own account. In Macedonia he procured one of the large harmless serpents found in that province and went back to his native town Abonotichus there to set up an "oracle factory," as Lucian calls it. At Chalcedon he secretly placed on a roadside a tablet bearing the inscription that the god Aesculapius, with his father, Apollo, was soon to be at Abonotichus; the finding of this tablet caused great excitement. Meanwhile Alexander, in his native place, went about with his long, curling locks falling over his shoulders, wearing a purple robe with white stripes, and armed with a sabre. His stupid fellow townsmen, though they knew his parents, who were poor, believed him when he claimed descent from Perseus, and when they heard of the tablet set about erecting a temple to Aesculapius. Between the foundation stones of the temple Alexander secretly placed a goose-egg shell containing a newly-hatched snake; then with the wild gesticulations of a god-inspired enthusiast, hastened to the market-place, and there announced 'to the people that Aesculapius had just been born at the temple in the form of a serpent. To prove his oracle true he held up before them the egg with the snake. On the publication of this wondrous news, the populace flocked to the market-place. Alexander had a hut of boards erected, within which he seated himself in a reclining chair; then taking up the large snake already mentioned, which he had kept out of sight, he laid it on his breast, drew over its head a linen mask, painted to resemble a human face, the mouth of which would open and shut on pulling a string, and gave out to the people that the newborn god had already grown to that great size, and was now ready to give oracles. From all Asia Minor and Thrace the people came in thousands to witness the miracle. The mystic semi-obscurity of the hut and the magical effects of artificial light magnified the impression that the charlatan and his snake made on the people. Whoever wished to receive an oracle of the god had to write his question on a tablet, which was then to be sealed with wax and handed to the prophet. When the people had retired he melted the seals, read the questions, wrote the answers, then sealed the tablets again, and gave them back (with the answers) the seals apparently intact. The tariff for oracles was a drachma and eight oboli (about 25 cents), and the annual receipts amounted to seventy or eighty thousand drachmas (say $15,000), but he had out of this sum to pay a host of assistants and confederates. When the temple was completed Alexander carried on his business there.

But his title to public regard did not pass unchallenged. The Epicureans, who detested all trickery, and who believed that enjoyment was the only end in life worth thinking of, manifested their hostility to the prophet, and were, in turn, denounced by him as atheists and Christians. To safeguard his reputation he added to his repertoire. First, he began to give oracles viva voce, a confederate behind a screen speaking the responses into a tube terminating at the mouth of the snake's mask. But the charge for such oracles was higher, and they were elicited only for the behoof of persons of eminence. Alexander's fame spread even to Rome, and dupes from that seat of enlightenment came to consult the serpent-god. One of these addle-pate pilgrims from Rome asked the oracle what manner of woman he should take to wife. The oracle named the daughter of Alexander; so he married her, and offered hecatombs to his mother in law, his bride's mother, in her capacity of moon-goddess, for such Alexander gave her out to be. Encouraged by many successes not inferior to this, the prophet instituted many mystic festivals, from which he excluded all unbelievers in God, as Epicureans and Christians. At these festivals the birth of Aesculapius and the nuptials of Alexander and the Moon-Goddess were represented dramatically, though perhaps a trifle too realistically. The prophet also claimed to be a reincarnation of Pythagoras, and in proof showed his thigh encased in gilded leather. His life was a continuous debauch. In time he began to hold what we should now call "dark seances;" that is, he would sit in absolute darkness and make 'response to questions submitted in writing on sealed tablets. As he could not read the questions at all, his answers (the oracles) were expressed for the most part in unintelligible language. Lucian once tested his powers by submitting to him the one question, "When will Alexander be caught at his tricks," written on eight tablets; he got eight different answers, all irrelevant He missed no opportunity of unmasking the rogue, and of teaching the people by the evidence of their own senses that the man was a vulgar impostor. The knave affected a mild friendship for his adversary, but he bribed the helmsman of a vessel on which Lucian sailed to throw him overboard; this the man had not the courage to do. Lucian wished to have the impostor put on trial for this crime, but the proconsul advised him not to invoke the help of the law, Alexander being too high in favor with the officials and the public. The city of Abonotichus had coins struck bearing the effigy of the Aesculapius serpent, and the pseudoprophet attained the age of seventy years, enjoying to the end the undiminished respect of the people.

Many were the impostors that sprang up after Alexander, and wherever there was any lack of real ones, fictitious pseudoprophets were imagined by satiric writers, Lucian's Peregrinus, for example, a renegade Christian who devotes himself to a death by fire to win fame. It was a mad world then. New mysteries were invented in plenty, and people came in crowds for initiation. The "Golden Ass" of Apuleius is a striking satire on this mystery furore. To this period belong the Gnostics', whose doctrines were a mixture of Judaism, heathenism and Christianity; the Manichees, who gave a Christian varnish to the Persian fire worship; the Kabbalists, who heaped a vast amount of rubbish together, got out of the Hebrew Bible by juggling with its sentences, words, letters and numbers. Amid this tangle of doctrines the heathen religions sank, Judaism lost its native land, and Christianism fell into an incalculable number of sects an evil that was not to be corrected even by the artificial unity of the Church under the Apostolical See.

PART SIXTH

The Knights Templar

1. The Middle Age

WITH THE SPREAD of Christianism the heathen mysteries came everywhere to an end, and the Christian mysteries took their place. The Christians, it is true, no longer constituted a secret society, after their faith had become the creed of the state; but there was plenty of mystic doctrine, nevertheless, and incessant strife of parties and sects, Arians and Athanasians, Pelagians and Semipelagians, Nestorians, Monophysites and Monothelites, Adoptionists, Priscillianists, and Donatists, to name no more, over Christ's nature, on the question whether the Holy Ghost proceeds only from the Father or equally from him and the Son; whether the soul is saved by good works or by grace of God, and so on interminably. This wrangling so occupied the minds of all that there was no longer need of secret societies. Theology, i. e., the struggle for creed, and war, i. e., the struggle for power, were the occupations of the Middle Age. Monks and knights were the two great classes of that time, with the Pope as supreme head on one side, and the Emperor on the other.

All the available knowledge was in the Middle Age employed in the service of the Church, and hence science slept from the migration of the barbarians till the invention of printing. During that period of a thousand years no addition was made to the sum of human knowledge. Arabian and Jewish physicians alone labored to save the intellectual wealth inherited from the ancient Greeks. As for Christendom, it was involved in profound intellectual darkness, and the Doctrine of Light that had been published by the Carpenter's Son, was lost amid petty controversies and inane interpretations, till at last its strictly monotheistic groundwork was forgotten, and there remained visible only the superstructure of ethnic mysticism and of doctrines, as the Trinity, Incarnation, Resurrection, and Ascension, borrowed from Egyptian and Grecian mythology.

And this ethnico-mystic structure acquired a splendor and a power never before equaled, so that the system was credited to divine intervention, whereas its purely human origin might easily have been traced. The root idea of the ethnic mysticism was to seek the supposedly "lost deity," to find him, to be unified with him. And the self-same idea underlay the Christian mysticism, and it was by calling that idea into play and by giving it expression in brilliant achievement, that this mysticism won its highest triumph, and, aided by the Papacy, its widest influence. This new embodiment of the mystical idea was seen in the Crusades, in which the Christian mystics joined, going forth to seek the lost sepulchre of their God, and to obtain control of it. Possession of the sepulchre would be the surest guarantee for the unification of godhead and humanity.

In this undertaking the two most powerful estates of the Middle Age took part the monks and the knights. The monks, under orders from the Pope, joined the armies of the cross; the knights, commanded by the Emperor, marched to the Holy Land and conquered it. After the conquest, when there was a kingdom of Jerusalem after the model of the kingdoms of the West, there arose, as the necessary summit of mediaeval aspiration, the union of monkery and chivalry, in the monkish orders of knights, whose members wore the sword of the knight and took the monastic vows of poverty, chastity, and obedience.

These organizations had their origin in the gradual assumption of knightly elements by the monastic orders. Some merchants of Amalfi, oldest commercial emporium of Italy, had, as early as 1048, founded a monastery and a church at Jerusalem, and in conjunction with these a hospital in honor of John the Baptist. There the monks cared for pilgrims who were poor or ailing. Pope Paschal II. granted them a monastic constitution in 1113, and Godfrey of Bouillon, soon after the capture of Jerusalem, endowed them with considerable properties.

They took the title of Brothers Hospitalers of Saint John of Jerusalem; their habit consisted of a black mantle with a white cross. A few years later (1119) the Knights Hugo of Payns, and Godfrey of Saint Omers, associated themselves and six other knights, all French, ini a military league, under the style "Poor Knights of Christ," pledging themselves to keep the highways of the Holy Land safe for pilgrims, and to observe the rule of Saint Benedict. The members were favored by King Baldwin I. and the Patriarch of Jerusalem, and came to be called Templars, because their convent stood on the site of the Solomonic Temple. The Templars received from the Synod of Troyes in 1128 recognition as a regular order, a monastic rule, a monastic habit, a special banner, etc. About the same date the Hospitalers, Johannites, or Knights of Saint John of Jerusalem, became invested with the knightly character. After the Hospitalers came the German Knights, whose theatre of action was principally the region of the Baltic Sea, but they also saw service in Spain in the war against the Saracens. Other knightly orders were those of Calatrava, of Alcantara, of Santiago de Compostella, in England the order of the Knights of the Holy Sepulchre, etc.

2. The Templars

NONE OF THESE orders rose to higher distinction than the order of the Templars, or of "the Poor Companions of the Temple of Jerusalem," as it was styled ini its rule. In those days it was full of the spirit of lowliness, but the time came when the knights were no longer called themselves "Poor Companions," but "Knights Templar." At first the brethren begged their bread, fasted, were diligent in attendance on divine worship, performed the duties of their religion, fed the poor, cared for the sick. Plain and unadorned was their attire, in color either black, white or brown; and the brother who tried to get the finest habit got the shabbiest. The hair and beard were close cropped. The chase was not permitted, except for the extermination of beasts of prey. Women were not allowed to live in the houses of the order; the brethren might not so much as kiss their female relations. But their mode of life became in time very different They became rich in worldly goods, and so broke the vow of poverty. As an order and as individuals they followed their own inclinations, and thus was their vow of obedience made nought; and their vow of chastity fared not better; while the specific vow of the order protection of pilgrims to the Holy Land became a nullity through their negligence, or even by their treasonable surrender of posts to the Saracens.

The candidate for admission to the order was required to be of noble birth, though sometimes illegitimate sons of knights were received. Furthermore, the candidate must be unmarried and unbetrothed; but this rule was circumvented by taking married candidates as "affiliate" members; they also admitted minors and even small boys. Lucre was the impelling motive of this disregard of their rule; money was their god. No other order of knights was in such disrepute for lewdness, duplicity, even treason. Originally all Templars were of one rank and degree that of knights. But in time ecclesiastics were admitted to attend to the spiritual affairs, and these ecclesiastics were made independent of the ordinary jurisdiction of diocesans. Thus was formed a second rank or degree, subordinate to the knights, and mere dummies on festival and ceremonial occasions. Then was added still another class, Servientes, who were the personal attendants of the knights, or were otherwise employed for the benefit of the order, as mechanics, laborers, etc. The class Affiliates comprised persons of all. ranks in life and of both sexes. They were not bound by all the vows of the order; they were required to make the order heir of their property; but they did not live in the houses of the order. These several classes were distinguished by their attire.

Knights wore a white mantle with an eight-pointed red cross over the left breast. Clerics wore the cassock, with brown mantle (the mantle of the higher clerics was white). Servientes wore a brown garb. The members called each other Brother, and indeed they stood by each other like brothers; in battle their personal bravery was irreproachable.

All these religious orders of knights possessed great power in the Middle Age, their grandmasters ranking next after Popes and monarchs. In fact they recognized no emperor or king as their lord, but only the Pope. The orders were favored by the Pontiffs, who loaded them with praise and privileges, though they feared them. If the Popes had now the arm of the flesh and not of the spirit only to defend them against the secular power, they owed that advantage to the knightly orders. And specially were they beholden to the Templars in this regard. The Templars were free from all Church tribute, and by the Pope's favor had the right to harbor excommunicated knights, to conduct divine service in churches that were under interdict, to found churches and churchyards; which privileges brought down upon them the enmity of the clergy. As the order was exempt from all episcopal jurisdiction and subject only to the Roman See, the bishops endeavored to have that and other like privileges abated by the Lateran Council in 1179. At the time of their suppression the Templars possessed an empire of five provinces in the East and sixteen in the West, with 15,000 houses of the order. In possession of such resources, they aimed at nothing short of making all Christendom dependent on their order, and to set up a sort of military aristocratic commonwealth, governed ostensibly by the Pope, but really by themselves, with their grandmaster at the head. The grandmaster of the Templars was elected by a college of eight knights, four servientes and one cleric. The Grandmaster was only president of the Council and its representative; but in war he had supreme command; as the Pope's deputy he had jurisdiction over the clerics. A splendid retinue attended him, and he had a treasury at his disposal. Next in rank after him stood the Seneschal, his' deputy for civil affairs, and the Marshal for military, the Treasurer, the Drapier. The Council (Conventus) consisted of the Grandmaster, his assistants (i.e., the grand officers just mentioned), Provincial Masters who might be present, and such knights as the Grandmaster might summon. By addition of all eminent Templars the Council became the General Chapter; this was the legislative body. The other knightly orders were organized on a plan not essentially different. What interests us most at present is those features of the Templar order which marked it as in some respects a secret society.

The order took its first steps in this direction in the thirteenth century, moved thereto by desire to safeguard its riches and power. Its secret doctrines or tenets were borrowed from the heretical sects of the time Albigenses and Waldenses or were such beliefs as were held in secret by many of the most enlightened men. Such views were shared by religious men, scholars, and worldlings alike, by the first class out of indignation against the moral degeneration of the rulers of the Church; by the second, because they suspected that the Church's dogmas were but inventions of Popes and councils, and by the third, because in rejecting the Church's authority and accepting the heretical doctrines, they fancied! that they were freed from the obligations of morality. But the Templars, who were neither pious nor learned, but of whom many were very worldly indeed, found the enlightened new opinions to coincide well with their interest, which prompted them to care rather for their numerous possessions in the West than for the few they held in lands occupied by the Moslem. God, said they, showed his favor to the Mohammedans in the Crusades, and evidently willed the defeat of the Christian arms. So by adopting the more enlightened views, they prepared the way for a withdrawal from the useless Crusades, and a return with bag and baggage to Europe, where they could rest from their glorious but hard and thankless martial labors, and devote themselves to the service of princes, or pass the time in the splendid houses of their order, amid Oriental luxury, and surrounded by gardens like Fairyland, beguiling the hours with gaming and the chase, with songs and lovemaking, the while not neglecting their political interests. But the Templars were rapidly nearing their downfall.

3. The Secrets of the Templars

THE ARCANA OF the Templars consisted of a secret doctrine and of a cult based on the same. The doctrine, which had no ground in scientific research, seems to have been akin to the doctrine of certain sects, specially the Albigenses, who worshiped a superior god of heaven and an inferior god of earth, and ascribed to the latter the origin of evil. For the Templars, Christ was no Son of God, had worked no miracles, had neither risen from the dead nor ascended into heaven; he was, in fact, often spoken of as a false prophet. The Church's doctrine regarding the transubstantiation of the bread in the mass was for them crass superstition, the eucharist only a commemorative rite, the sacrament of penance a priestly imposture, the Trinity a human invention, veneration of the cross an act of idolatry. That the opposition of the order to the last-mentioned custom led on festival occasions, and particularly when new members were admitted, to overt acts of contempt for the cross, to spitting on the 'cross, for example accusations like that are grave not only from the point of view of the Church, but even of common propriety, and they played an important part in the prosecution of the Templars. That postulants were compelled by force of arms and other violent means to perform such highly reprehensible acts is not to be discredited entirely, for they may have been part of a test of the postulants' willingness to obey superiors: and besides, the objectionable ceremony was not practiced everywhere, but only in France. More excusable was the offense of the Templars in looking on the cross broidered on their mantle, not as the sign of redemption, but as a double T, the initial letter of the name of their society. They were said also to have substituted John the Baptist in the place of Jesus as the order's patron, because John did not pretend to miraculous powers nor declare himself the Messiah. The clerics of the order must have approved these heretical opinions and practices. There were at that time many enlightened churchmen, and it is to be presumed that the Templars would adopt such of them as were at variance with the hierarchy and took refuge in the order.

The Templars' secret rites, introduced in the middle of the thirteenth century, were practiced as part of their peculiar religious service, and at the admission of new members: for though the Catholic liturgy was used in their chapels, the initiated performed a: cult of their own in the chapter house, or chapel, before break of day. This consisted of confession and communion, as understood by Templars. This confession they regarded on the one hand as an act of brotherly trust, and on the other of brotherly counsel: hence, they confessed only to the chaplains of the order; in the latter times of the order the members were forbidden to confess to priests that were not Templars. By them the communion was taken in the natural species and substance of bread and wine, and in token of brotherly love, not as commemorative of any sacrifice.

Two images played a part in the Templar rites. The image of John the Baptist typified the order's opposition to the Church's creed. The other image, jealously guarded from the eyes of outsiders, has been called an "idol." It was made chiefly of copper, gilt, and represented now a human skull, anon the countenance of an old man heavily bearded (makroprosopos), again a very small face (mikroprosopos), which would be now the face of a man, then of a woman, anon male and female at once; it would have now one, again two or three, heads, with bright shining eyes of carbuncles. The idol was by some Templars called "Bassomet," but why, does not appear. From the statements of members of the order it would seem that this idol was a kind of talisman that brought all manner of good fortune; that it was set up for veneration as rival to the cross, and that they called it "the savior of the order."

There were two forms of admission, the general and the special (or secret) form: the latter was used only at the admission of postulants that could be trusted with the secrets of the order. The Scribe, acting as Receptor, first asked the brethren, in chapter, if they had any objection to make the admission of the postulant. If none objected the postulant was led into an adjoining room and questioned as to his purpose in seeking entrance to the order, whether h'e knew of any impediment on his part, whether he owed debts that he could not pay, whether he was married or engaged to be married, and so forth. The questions having been satisfactorily answered, and the minutes of the replies reported to the brethren, the matter was again put to vote. Next, the candidate was brought before the chapter, and, after more questioning, took the vows and was formally admitted. In the secret rite of admission the Receptor showed to the candidate the Idol, with these words: "Believe in this, put your trust in this, and all will be well with you." Then he girded the candidate with a cord of white wool fibres, the Baptist's girdle, as it was called, which he was to wear over the shirt. The obligation of secrecy was very sternly enforced. Those who betrayed any of the secrets of the order were cast into prison, and the candidate was threatened with dungeons and death should he communicate to an outsider any information about the ceremony of initiation.

Thus did the Templars, an order instituted for the purpose of guarding the Church's interests, in the end reject the Church's doctrines, and adopt principles that tended inevitably to the overthrow, not only of the Papacy, but of Christianism itself. Such was the irreconcilable opposition between the avowed and the 'secret convictions of the Templars, and such was the hypocrisy of the order: for, though they had apostatized from the creeds of the Church, they would not formally quit her communion; and though they regarded as true many points of anti-Christian doctrine, they veiled these with mystery, or even on occasion made sport of them, instead' of publishing them, as so many poor, unarmed heretics did; and hence their aspirations were foiled, and the most powerful association of that time perished, not in glorious battle, but in ignominious dungeons and at the stake.

4. The Downfall of the Knights Templar

THE CRUSADES HAVING failed utterly, the Holy Land having again come under the power of the "infidels," and the occupation of the knightly orders having gone, the Popes cast about for a remedy for this undesirable state of things. The order of German Knights had already forestalled the problem by choosing as their theatre of action the countries on the Baltic Sea, and the Spanish orders by waging continual wars against the Moors; and the Knights of Saint John (Hospitalers) later found a place for themselves by occupying Rhodes. But the Templars were without any fit employment, and that circumstance was the occasion of their downfall. About the year 1305 Pope Clement V. proposed a union of the Templars with the

Hospitalers, and, if possible, with other orders, but both Templars and Hospitalers rejected the advice.

Philip IV. (the Fair) of France found in the Templars a serious obstacle to his ambition, and in the early years of his reign sought to compel them by force to aid him in his schemes; but failing in that design, tried to win them by loading them with favors. Many different explanations have been offered to account for another change of policy on the part of Philip, but none of them is historically sound* Probably the change noticeable in the king's attitude toward the order in 1305 was in some way connected with the outrageous doings of the Inquisition in the South of France; doubtless rumors of heresy in the Templar order had come to the omnipresent ear of the Holy Court. The Inquisitor-General of France, William Imbert, prior of the Dominicans in Paris, begged the King to call the Templars to account. The King, on Nov. 14, 1305, informed Clement V. of the accusation, but Clement, notwithstanding this, invited not only the Grandmaster of the Hospitalers, but also the head of the Templars, to meet with himself in conference about the project of a new Crusade. Yet in his letter to the Templars' Grandmaster, James Molay (who resided in his palace in Cyprus), he counseled him to come without escort, "lest the news of his departure should give occasion to enemies (of the order) to make a sudden onslaught." The Master of the Hospitalers was unable to come, being busied with the siege of Rhodes, and Molay, contrary to the Pope's advice, came to France escorted by his entire council, sixty knights, and bringing the treasure and the archives of his order. In May, 1307, the Pope and the King met at Poictiers, and, it is supposed, discussed thoroughly the question of the Templars: about the same time the Templars informed the Pope of the dangers that threatened them, and asked for an investigation of the charges brought against them: such investigation the Pope decided to institute. It cannot be determined whether it was with the Pope's approval, or against his wishes, that Philip on Oct. 13, 1307, had all the Templars in France arrested and their goods seized.

Five heads of complaint were alleged against the order; viz., profanation of the cross, worship of an idol, indecent rites of initiation, omission of the sacramental words (i.e., the words of consecration or of transubstantiation, Hoc est corpus meum) in masses performed by priests belonging to the order, and indulgence of unnatural lusts. Two days after the arrests the people of Paris, whose partiality for the Templars was feared, were assembled before the royal palace, and there were labored with by monks and royal officials, to turn them against the order. The King took up his residence in the "Temple," the Paris house of the order, in which was hid the treasure of the Grandmaster (150,000 gold florins, and twelve horse-loads of silver pence). It was not quite 500 years later when the Temple became the prison of a descendant of the King. In that same building, in presence of the masters and bachelors of the university, the trial of the Grandmaster and his brethren was commenced, and proceeded under the direction of Imbert. The procedure was the same as in the ordinary trials for heresy and witchcraft in the court of the Inquisition. Confessions were obtained by use of the torture, and it is impossible at this day to tell how much in those confessions was due to the employment of that peculiar method of eliciting truth, and how much, if any part, was prompted by the desire to atone for past offenses by truthful (even if forced) admission of guilt.

The Pope was not pleased with this turn of affairs. He claimed for himself the right to proceed against the Templars, declared that the King was infringing the privileges of the See of Rome, and attributed the action taken against the Templars to a desire to get possession of the order's treasury and to annihilate a society whose existence was a cause of anxiety to the King. He, therefore, protested against the whole proceeding, and demanded that the arrested Templars and their property should be surrendered to him as judge of the questions at issue. The King refused, but he came to an understanding with the Pope in the matter of the prosecution, and Nov. 22 the Pope, by the bull "Pastoralis Praeeminentiae," ordered the arrest of all the Templars throughout the Christian world. The King of England, Edward II. who was Philip's son-in-law, obeyed this precept, though he had previously expressed disbelief of the guilt of the Templars. A like change of mind was seen in Aragon. In Cyprus the Templars attempted resistance, but submitted. Denis, King of Portugal, refused to institute a prosecution against them.

Inasmuch as the measure was one that affected all countries, the case of the Templars belonged of right to the Papal jurisdiction. Even Philip admitted this; but he mistrusted the Pope, and feared that the Templars might be acquitted, and then take revenge on the King. Negotiations were opened. The King demanded the death of the Templars, but the Pope would not consent to this till their guilt was fully proven; and again he demanded the surrender to him of their persons and their possessions. The King at last acceded to the demand, for he had need of the Pope's assistance in procuring the election of his brother as successor to the assassinated German King, Albert. Under the Papal jurisdiction the trials were conducted with more lenity: torture was not employed. But the Pope became convinced of the guilt of the accused; till then he had been in doubt. Molay made, without compulsion, many very important admissions, as did several high officials of the order, but on sundry points they contradicted one another. Nevertheless, the Pope was still firmly of the opinion that only individual Templars were on trial, not the order, while for the King the annihilation of the order was the main thing. August 8, 1308, the bull "Faciens Misericordiam" ordered a prosecution of the Templars in every country of Christendom; and on the 12th of the same month, by the bull "Regnans in Coelis," a council was summoned for the year 1310, to determine the question of the Templars. Further ordinances of the Pope had to do with the surrender of the properties of the order to the Church.

Meanwhile the Pope had forgotten to aid the French King's brother in his pretentions to the crown of the Roman Empire. On the contrary, he favored the election of Henry VII. of Luxemburg, and was glad to find in him a prince who would strenuously oppose the overweening ambition of Philip IV. The tension between the Pope and the French King was increasing, and the trials of the Templars went on sluggishly for two years more. There was much arbitrary ill-usage of Templars. The bishops, to whom the Pope had committed the prosecution of the individual members of the order, in many places gave loose rein to their ancient enmity toward the Templars, and freely used the torture; nevertheless, very many of the accused maintained the innocence of their order, and declared the prior confessions false. This can be explained only by supposing that the abuses in the order did not extend to all the houses. Molay's behavior on his trial was neither firm nor dignified, ever balancing between self-accusation and vindication. He was never sure of his ground, sought to retard procedure, used equivocal and obscure phrases, and continually protested his orthodoxy; and the other members for the most part acted in like manner: but their excuse is the hard usage they endured, and Molay was not permitted to complain of that.

All the Templars arrested in Paris, numbering 546, were on the 28th of May, 1310, mustered in the garden of the Bishop's palace, and there the accusation was read to them. Six of the accused three knights and three clerics protested in the name of all against the treatment they had received, and demanded the release of all Templars and arrest of their accusers. In vain! During the investigation thirty-six members of the order died in prison at Pans. May 12, 1310, those who had retracted their confessions, to the number of 54, were burned alive: to these were afterward added eight more, and at Rheims nine met the same fate: they all protested their innocence at the supreme moment. It is worthy of note that the Pope, who till then had favored delay in the proceedings, was now for instant action. He sharply reproved the English authorities for refusing to employ the torture; and he did his best to accomplish the destruction of the Templars at Avignen, who had taken up arms to defend themselves; but, though defeated, they were adjudged innocent; and it was the same in Castile. In Germany, where the order, though weak in numbers, made a resolute stand, the Pope offered no convincing proof of the charges; and in England, too, nothing could be proved against the accused members. But throughout the greater part of Italy the Templars fared as in France, except that they were not condemned to the stake. In vain did the celebrated Raymond Lully, at the Council of Vienne (1312), plead for the preservation of the order by a consolidation of all the military orders in one, whose Grandmaster should be that French prince who happened to be King of Jerusalem: for he hoped thus to conciliate the good will of Philip. The Pope, who had long been urged by the King to suppress the ofder, now made haste to save the property of the Templars from falling into secular hands, and so, by the bulls "Vox in Excelso" and "Ad Providam Christi Vicarii," published April 3 and May 2, 1312, respectively, he made over to the Hospitalers all the estates of the Templars, estates in Spain excepted.

The unfortunate Grandmaster Molay, who received a pittance of four sous per diem to alleviate his misery, bore his imprisonment with great fortitude; but March n, 1313, he and Godfrey de Charney, an official of the order, having retracted their confessions, were slowly burnt to death on an island in the Seine, by order of the King, without any judicial process. Molay, it is said, cited the two murderers of his brethren, Philip and Clement, to appear before the judgment seat of God. They both died, one of colic, the other in consequence of a fall from his horse, eight and thirteen months, respectively, after the death of Molay. The order was suppresed everywhere except in Portugal, where it took the name "Order of Jesus Christ," and continued in existence. Its Grandmaster, Prince Henry the navigator, a hundred years afterward, employed its wealth in promoting the high ends of civilization. In other countries the Templars either wandered about as fugitives or entered the order of Hospitalers. The seizure of the order's estates in France was annulled by the bull of suppression, but Philip, nevertheless, maintained his hold on the house of the order in Paris, and on the treasure there stored. The remainder of the property was plundered by the nobility and the Church; and the Pope surely was not forgetful of his own interest. The Hospitalers afterward succeeded to their rights, but that did them hardly less harm than good, for it cost them a great sum to release the estates of the Templars from the grasp of the robbers; besides, many a small piece of property was made away with by princes, great lords, orders, churches, and monasteries.

PART SEVENTH
The Femgerichte

1. Courts of Justice in the Middle Age

THE WILD DISORDER attending the irruption of the Gothic nations having subsided, society, which had lost its bearings, had to organize itself anew. The first step toward this end was taken when society's task was distributed among innumerable fractional parts of itself, each fraction trying to do its own share of the work; the next step was the uniting of all these fractional parts under one religious idea that of Christianism, and under one political law that of feudalism. The Pope and the Emperor represented the religious and the political ideas respectively. As long as one was true to Pope and Emperor i.e., was a good Christian and a good subject all was well with him, and he might, in all other matters, do as he pleased. The principle of Justice was not regarded: no wrong act was punished as violating right, but always as doing harm. Even murder was not regarded as infringement of human right to life, but simply as harm done to the people of the murdered one. If one was without relatives, his slayer went unpunished; but if the murdered man left a family or kinsmen, the murderer, on paying to them a certain sum, went forth free. Thus, the utmost unrestraint prevailed in the several small aggregations of people, and the utmost diversity between one little community and another. Of bureaucratic, centralized, cast-iron government there was no faintest foreshadow; nor was government a function assigned to anyone, but, like the administration of justice, an acquired right. In a given province this one had acquired the government, that one the civil and a third the criminal judiciary; one was obeyed in peace, another commanded the people in war. Jurisdictions were undefined and inextricably mixed up a consequence of the feudal system, under which the King granted rights now to one man, again to another, as favors, never inquiring how these might consist with rights previously granted to others. In this way it became possible in the Middle Age for such juristic abnormities as the Femgerichte to come into existence. The Femgerichte resulted from the confusion existing in judiciary affairs, just as the religious abnormity of the monastic orders of knights resulted from the very opposite condition of things in the Church the excess of regulation. For the confusion (absence of regulation) and the excessive regulation were near akin; they both sprang out of the unrestraint of private life in the Middle Age, which unrestraint naturally produced, under the rule of the Church, a multitude of monastic rules (e.g., the Rule of St. Augustin, of St. Benedict, of St. Columba, etc.); while, on the contrary, the feebleness of the Empire, due to the jealousy of the Popes and the ambition and avarice of the feudal lords, was fatal to any organization of the administrative and judicial functions, and though there were many codes of law, there could be no standard for distinguishing right and wrong.

The cause of this difference of development between State

and Church was, that the Church had grown from the top downward, from the hierarchy down to the people; while the State, on the contrary, had grown from below upward. During the process of migration and settlement, each nation or horde was self-governed, perfectly free and independent: hence, the popular, genial, oftentimes even jovial and humorous cast of Teutonic law, as compared with the hard, pedantic, abstruse, austere character of the Jus Romanum. Roman law has only a corpus juris; Teutonic law has Wise Saws, Juristic Proverbs, Juristic Drolleries, Juristic Myths (Weistuemer, Rechtssprichtwoerter, Rechtsschwoernke, Rechtssagen).

Originally, among the Germans, the freemen themselves were the court and chose their president, the Graf (graf now equals count). Not until the time of Karl the Great (Charlemagne) did the grafs become standing officials, and later an hereditary order and lords proprietary. As the functions of government were by degrees entrusted to fewer and ever fewer hands, being transferred from the people to favored feudal lords, and from them passing finally into the hands of an individual sovereign a quite natural process, for while the people increased in number they did not become better educated, and therefore grew ever less fitted for self-government so, too, judgment, quitting the open, embowered courts amid the lindens, with heaven's breezes whispering among the leaves, and heaven's blue dome overarching all, withdrew behind dank and frowning walls, from the countenance of the whole people to a meeting of a small bench of stern judges.

Thus gradually were the rights of the freemen diminished. The freemen was less and less frequently called to sit in judgment, for the president of the court, the graf. was no longer an equal, but a great lord, their superior, who made up the court as to him seemed best, and who even cared nothing for the Emperor.[*]

Westphalia was the original home of the Femgerichte, and they owed their rise to the fact that there the royal ban (Koenigsbann), that is to say, the right possessed by the King alone, of conferring the grafship on the grafs, was still alive, in modified form indeed, yet with its substance unimpaired. Owing to the granting of various privileges to ecclesiastical and secular magnates the jurisdiction of the grafs was in time divided up. Besides, there were special courts for freemen, and special courts for the half-free and the unfree, the former courts being under the free grafs, and the other under the ga-ugrafafs (district grafs). Now, as the majority of the population were under the gaugrafs, the possession of a gaugrafship developed into sovereignty; while the position of the free grafs became peculiar: the office was often sold and passed from hand to hand. The free grafs, who were often persons of little means, in order to maintain their dignity, had to lean on the King's ban, or warrant, obtainable from the King alone. But often the free grafships died out, or they were consolidated with gaugrafships. But nowhere did they retain so much of their original character as in Westphalia a geographical expression of various meanings, indeed, but in general it denoted the region between the Rhine and the Weser. The term Freigraf dates from the twelfth century.

---

[*] What folows regarding the Femgerichte is based on Theodor Lindner's work, "Die Femgerichte," Münster and Paderborn, 1888. (Whatever may have been the original meaning of the word "fem" in "femgericht," it is enough to know that in usage it is equivalent to "secret"; hence fem-gericht secret Judgment, or secret tribunal.)

Not only the King but the duke also had influence over the free grafships. After the break-up of the ancient duchy of Saxony, every princely land proprietor within its territory was duke of Westphalia; this is specially true of the Archbishop of Cologne, and also of the bishops of Muenster, Osnabrueck and Minden, and of the Duke of Saxe-Lauenburg dukes of Westphalia all, but with more or less limitation. Probably the duke was entitled to preside over any free court, and to summon to his own tribunal, the "botding," the free grafs. So, too, the stuhlherr (lord of the manor) possessed the right of presiding, even when he was no prince, but only a graf; and often he assumed that the free graf gave judgment only in his (the lord's) name, and so granted release from the jurisdiction of the free courts, to cities, for example. The free graf and his assessors, the schoeffen (a lower grade of judges), afterward called freischoeffen, constituted the freigericht (free court), afterward known as femgericht. These offices might fall to any freeman and any one was reckoned a freeman who had "his own smoke," i. e., a house of his own.

In the latter half of the 14th and the first half of the 15th century the emperors bestowed on the archbishops of Cologne, as dukes of Westphalia and lieutenants of the Emperor, the right of investiture of all free grafs and supervision of them all over Westphalia, A chapter of free grafs was held yearly at Arnsberg, and hence the Arnsberg tribunal obtained the first rank.

As the free grafs held their investiture from the king, they looked on themselves as king's officers, and little by little went on extending their jurisdiction over the whole empire a design favored by the confusion reigning everywhere, and even approved by the emperors themselves. At last the free grafs began to think that they were higher than the emperor, and had no need of his meddling: this arrogance was at its height in the reign of Sigmund, and it was still to be seen under Frederic VII.; in fact, Frederic, for having taken steps to punish some insubordinate free grafs, was summoned by free grafs to stand trial.

Some of the emperors did, indeed, set up free graf tribunals outside the limits of Westphalia; but these never prospered. In the 15th century it was an axiom that such courts could exist only in Westphalia, or, as the saying was, "on red earth," a phrase that does not occur prior to 1490, and the sense of which is not quite clear; for neither is the soil of all Westphalia red, nor is red soil confined to Westphalia: and the same criticism may be made if "red earth" be taken for "blood-stained earth."

2. The Secret Tribunal

THE EARLY "FREE COURTS" were in a certaim sense "private" courts, inasmuch as they were not open to all like the courts of the gau-grafs (or judges of districts). The associate judges (Freischoeffen) were called "wissende" (wisemen, knowing ones), which, in old times meant "judges." The "private" tribunal of the Feme became by degrees a "secret" tribunal about the middle of the 14th century, as the free grafs became more conscious of their ambitious aims.

The Schoeffen were now required to bind themselves by oath to observe secrecy: the one who proved false to his oath was first to have his tongue plucked out, and then he was to be hanged, either three or seven feet higher than a thief. The penalty was exacted very rarely, and probably never the first item of it. The obligation of secrecy extended over all the proceeding's of the secret courts, even their letters and summonses. But the most important secret was the countersign, by means of which the initiated recognized each other. This was made up of four words (taken from the oath), Stock, Stein, Gras, Grein; and as the words were pronounced one laid his right hand on the others' left shoulder. Poetry and romance have made the Feme courts sit in subterranean chambers, at night, the faces of the judges masked. The fact is that the tribunals of the Feme were set up at the ancient seats of the free tribunals, and of such places there were in Westphalia more than a hundred; and the trials were always held in the open air, in broad daylight Whether in certain cases they were also public, so that any one might be present, is not known. In all cases where testimony was taken the proceedings were secret; whoever willingly or unwillingly was present unbidden at the secret deliberations was straightway hanged from the nearest tree.

Very remarkable was the universal recognition throughout Germany of the power of the Femgerichte. In 1387 the most distinguished people of Cologne were "wissende"; about 1420 the Rhineland was full of wissende belonging to every grade in society; and soon after the same might be said of Bavaria, Tyrol, Switzerland, Suabia, Franconia, Saxony, Prussia. Every manor lord and every free city needed the advice of wissende. Princes and cities had their judges admitted as schoeffen; archbishops and princes, even the Emperor Sigmund, were initiated: in the middle of the 15th century there must have been more than 100,000 freischoeffen in the empire. To be initiated became a craze, a fad; the native Westphalians were amazed at the folly of their southern and eastern countrymen.

And the long arm of the Femgericht jurisdiction reached as far as the host of wissende: the localities in which the activity of the secret tribunals was manifested were scattered all over the empire; in fact, the proceedings of these courts which affected Westphalia itself became a very small fraction of the whole.

But with the spread of the Feme jurisdiction arose opposition to the same. There were seen faint beginnings of opposition even in the early part of the 14th century, when Bremen decided not to allow members of the Feme courts to reside within its jurisdiction; toward the close of that century other cities took more effective measures, and in the 15th were even formed leagues of cities for self-defense against the encroachments of the Feme. Brunswick appealed to the Pope and the Emperor, and Hildesheim and Erfurt to the Council of Basel. In the middle of the 15th century several cities, especially in Southern Germany and in Holland, were freed from the jurisdiction of the secret courts by the supreme ecclesiastical and civil authorities. Then the dukes of Bavaria and of Saxony forbade their subjects laying complaints in the Westphalian courts and some cities punished that offense with death, imprisonment, or banishment.

A Feme court consisted of a free graf and! at least seven schoeffen. The graf was required to be a freeborn Westphalian of stainless reputation, whatever his station in life, for peasants were often chosen to be grafs. The schoeffen also had to be freemen born, and if not of Westphalian birth, were required to present proofs of their fitness. There was a fee for admission to the Feme. As time went on the examination of applicants became less and less strict, and often very questionable characters, even serfs and men accused of crimes, were admitted: such admissions were illegal, and the men chosen under such circumstances were called notschoeffen (makeshift schoeffen).

The free graf sat at a judgment-board, on which lay a naked sword and a rope as symbols of avenging justice, and the schoeffen took oath on these instruments. Each free graf and each schoeffe of a given court was required not only to be present at a trial, but to take part in pronouncing sentence. When the trial was one of special importance several hundred schoeffen would be in attendance.

The Femgerichte had their special codes and statutes, which were from time to time amended. In these the competence of the courts was defined, and this had to do iwith matters purely criminal, at least so far as the trials were held in secret. The crimes of which the Femgerichte took cognizance vemewrogige punkte (points for femic animadversion) were, according to the list drawn up at Dortmund in 1430, as follows: 1, robbery and acts of violence against ecclesiastics or churches; 2, larceny; 3, robbery of a woman in childbed or of a dying person; 4, plundering the dead; 5, arson and murder; 6, treachery; 7, betrayal of the Feme; 8, rape; 9, forgery of money or of title to property; 10, robbery on the imperial highway; 11, perjury and perfidy; 12, refusal to appear in court on summons. Apostasy from the Christian faith was put at the head of the list in an assembly held at Arnsberg 1437, and in 1490 heresy and witchcraft were added. For the person found guilty, there was but one punishment, death, and only one manner of death, by the rope. This penalty could be inflicted without sentence if the offender were taken in the act, or if he confessed guilt, or if there were eyewitnesses of the crime.

That among the offenses punishable by the Feme heresy and witchcraft held almost the first place shows that these tribunals were no object of apprehension to the ecclesiastical power. This secret association, therefore, differed from that of the Templars, as also from that of the Stonemasons (which will be next considered) especially in this, that the Feme was no league of Illuminati, but that their specialty was opposition to the law of the stronger and to the rule of petty states, and that their aim was to uphold and exaggerate antiquated judicial institutions.

The procedure of the Femgerichte was entirely in accord with the principle of ancient Teutonic law, that "where no complainant appears, neither is there any judge." It was not the inquisitorial court procedure of the 16th- 19th centuries, in which the judge made investigation on his own account, but a procedure founded entirely in the practice of civil courts, and one that agreed well with the independent spirit of the Middle Age, and the view that then prevailed that law was a matter of personal rights.

The free tribunals took up the complaint from whatever quarter it came. All schoeffen, too, were under obligation to bring to the attention of the free courts, and to prosecute all doings coming under the animadversion of the Feme. Hence were a schoeffe to give information regarding such offenses to any other court, he was

Hable to be hanged; and the same fate befel the one who, having been entrusted with a bill of accusation, should open the same and betray its contents. Accusations were not entertained unless when submitted by wissende. The accuser had to stand betwixt two fellow schoeffen, his sponsors, in front of the tribunal in kneeling posture. In every case the first thing done was to decide whether the crime was one meet for animadversion by the Feme. That decided, the accused was summoned to appear, if he was a wissender, before the secret tribunal, if not a wissender, before the open court. The first summons to a wissender to appear before the secret tribunal was drawn up in writing by two schoeffen, and allowed the accused a delay of six weeks and three days. If he did not obey the summons, then four schoeffen summoned him in person; and this proving-ineffectual, six schoeffen and one free graf repeated the summons, which now was called the "warning." The delay allowed was the same as at first. If the accused was a free graf the number of schoeffen employed in each of the three processes of summoning was 7, 14 and 21, respectively, and of free grafs 2, 4 and 7. The schoeffe, on receiving the summons, could appear at any time within the three delays before the free court and demand a statement of the charges and the names of the accusers; then he might on his sword swear to his innocence, and obtain his freedom; but he was liable to be summoned again. Outsiders were summoned once only, and usu-ally by only one schoeffe. When the whiereabouts of an accused person was unknown, four summonses were prepared, and these were posted in four places where he might possibly be found. If the accused was one who inspired fear, the summons might in the night time be posted or left at the gate of the castle or of the city m which he lived. In such cases the schoeffen walked or rode up before the gate, hacked off the crossbeam three chips, which they kept, put a penny of the realm in the notch, affixed the summons, and cried out to the castellan or the burgomaster, "We have stuck a king's brief in the notch and taken the proof with us: say you to him that is in the castle that he must on his appointed day present himself before the free tribunal, on behalf of highest law and the Emperor's ban." When the opposition to the Femgerichte began to gain force, the summoners were in greater peril often than the summoned: often they lost their lives.

The day of the trial having arrived, if the accuser was not on hand the accused was discharged. But if the accused failed to appear, the accusation was repeated and testimony taken. The free graf then thrice called the accused by name, and asked if anyone was there as his attorney. If there was no appearance of the accused, the accuser could demand judgment "after a se'ennight." In making this demand, he knelt, laid two fingers of the right hand on his naked sword, affirmed the guilt of the accused, and six schoeffen, as his sponsors, maintained the truth of what he swore. If the verdict was against the accused, the free graf arose, and outlawed the accused, in words like these: "The accused (name and surname) I except from the peace, the laws and the freedom (of the empire) as the same have been stablished and decreed by popes and emperors; and I cast him down and place him in uttermost unquiet and disgrace, and make him illegitimate, banned, outside the peace, dishonored, insecure, loveless; and I do outlaw him according to the sentence of the secret tribunal, and devote his neck to the rope, his carcass to the birds and beasts to devour; and I commend his soul to the power of God in heaven; and his fiefs and goods I give up to the lords of whom the fiefs are held; and I make his wife a widow and his children orphans." Then the free graf threw a twisted crd out over the bounds of the court, the schoeffen spat out, and the name of the outlaw was written in the book of the condemned. Among the persons thus condemned were numbered some men of high station, as the dukes Henry and Louis of Bavaria (1429), John, bishop of Wurtzburg, and others. All free grafs and schoeffen were henceforth under obligation to arrest and to execute sentence upon the outlaw (but three members of the Feme were required); and executing sentence meant hanging the culprit from the nearest tree. Often the relatives of executed outlaws of the Feme accused the executioners in the free courts as assassins, and the court could outlaw its own ministers for carrying out its own decrees. Many were the abuses that arose, assassination) of innocent persons, for example. Murderers, too, pretended to be schoeffen; and highwaymen robbed under pretense of sequestering the property of persons condemned by judgment of the Feme.

If ever the condemned, being a wissender and not having over-stayed the se'ennight of grace, appeared in court with six compurgators he was set free; but if he confessed his guilt, or was convicted, he was executed forthwith in the usual way. The ban of the Feme could never be lifted; but the number of death sentences actually carried out was, says Lindner, "so very small that one might readily allow the Feme's decree of outlawry to be pronounced upon him." Pope Nicolas V. in 1452 condemned the capital executions done by the Feme.

If a man under sentence of death should be proved innocent before he fell into the hands of the executioners, he was, if a wissender, brought before the court, with a rope around his neck, wearing white gloves, carrying a green cross, and attended by two schoeffen; falling on his knees before the free graf he pleaded for mercy. The free graf, taking him by the hand, bade him rise, removed the rope from around his neck, and restored him to the grace and favor of the Feme. But one who was not a wissender had no rights! He merely escaped death, but there was no amend. The Emperor gave him "a reprieve of 100 years, 6 weeks and a day" that was all; he was forever ineligible to become a schoeffe. Both processes were called the "entfemung" ("unfeming," undoing of the Feme's judgment).

Many of the condemned, unable to procure the entfemung, ventured to appeal to the Emperor, the camera, the Pope, or a Church Council. But the Femgerichte never recognized such appeals, and protested strongly to the Emperor against them. They regarded the condemned as dead, and said that no one had the right "to awaken the dead." The Emperor Sigmund could think of no means of saving a man under condemnation, except by taking him into his own service, for the Femgerichte did not care to take measures against officials of the Kaiser and the empire. Women, too, as well as aged men and children, were excepted from the cognizance of the Feme, also, in theory, Jews, for Jews were ""servants of the Emperor's bedchamber"; ecclesiastics, also, for they could in the Middle Age be tried only in the spiritual courts; but in the 15th century the Feme disregarded these provisions, and summoned) both' Jews and ecclesiastics.

3. The End of the Feme

BUT THE INITIATES of the Red Earth league met the fate that overtakes all movements that lag behind the times. The Feme did by no means render in the days of "faustrecht" (fist-right, the rule of the stronger) so great services as it has been credited with: never was the insecurity of life and property so great as when the Femgerichte were most flourishing. If the extension of the Feme beyond the borders of Westphalia was a wrong, that wrong became aggravated through the excessive secrecy of the tribunals. The Feme degenerated steadily, and the respect in which it was held declined in equal degree. The free grafs forgot the fair promise of their original institution that their function was to protect innocence against the machinations of bad men. They, and especially the presidents of courts, enriched themselves with feco for admission of new members, with costs of court, with fines and fees, and even with moneys got by extortion and oppression. They delayed trials, condemned innocent persons, overstepped the limits of their jurisdiction so as to condemn to death the entire male population (over 18 years) of a town, for not obeying a summons. The opposition to the Femgerichte culri mated in the decree of the Emperor Maximilian I. creating the supreme court of judicature (kammergericht), which left no further excuse for protecting the free courts. The applications for admission to the Feme soon grew less, and at last ceased. The princes changed the free courts into ordinary tribunals, or abolished them. At the end of the i6th century a capital execution by a Femgericht was a thing unknown; at the end of the 17th these courts had nearly all disappeared. But even when Westphalia was a Napoleonic kingdom there were still living some schoeffen, and not till the decade 1880-90 did the last free graf disappear, "taking with him to the grave the secret of the countersign." The existence of the Feme is still commemorated by the stone judgment seats under the lindens; and the branches overhead are still whispering the story of the redoubtable Wissende of the Red Earth country.

Stonemasons' Lodges of the Middle Ages

1. Medieval Architecture

We have already noted as a prominent characteristic of the Middle Age this, that freedom of action, except so far as it interfered with the interests of the clergy or the nobles, was left unrestricted and that individuals formed social unions for the exercise of it. Thus we have seen these two dominant classes uniting to form associations which finally were crowned by the institution of the military orders. But the medieval world had not followed the arts of peace very long after the stormy times of the barbarian invasions, before it became conscious of a need not only of a union of swordsmen and penmen, but also and still more of a union of handicraftsmen. True, the Middle Age could not rise to such an intellectual height as would enable it to see that work is more to be honored than indolence, peace than war: hence the worker had to take a subordinate place. Of the agricultural laborer this is true without any reservation: but the artisan was more favorably situated as soon as the cities had begun to develop.

But the progress made by the artisans was due to their union in corporations or gilds. The constitutions of the trade gilds derive partly from the "collegia" of artisans in ancient Rome and partly from the monastic orders. The "collegia" had secret rites, mysteries, but of these we have no reliable information; and it is certain that the medieval gilds had their mysteries, too. Of not all the gilds is this true; in some of them the secret ceremonial consisted only of passwords and countersigns by which craftsmen recognized their fellows. The most elaborate of these mysteries was that of the Stonemasons. And the reason if this is obvious, for of all trades that of the builder not only makes most demands on the thinking faculty, involves most details, is the first to require new methods of facilitating operations, new "wrinkles," and these easily are made trade secrets: besides, as builders of temples, the masons acquired a sacred and mystical character.

After the great migrations the mason's trade had its home in the monasteries. As long as architecture or the builder's art was thus under monastic guidance, it affected the Romanic style simple columns, rounded arches, squat towers; but when the monks forsook art and science, in the nth and 12th centuries, the craftsmen no longer saw why they should serve under the direction of men who had no taste for anything but wine, the chase, and war. And so there arose unions of masons outside of the monasteries, especially in the cities, and henceforth the monastic churches were inferior to the city churches in size and splendor. The change in the circumstances of the builders' unions, which were now self-controlled, was seen in the development of a new style. Instead of the single columns rose clustered columns, symbol of free union, and of the strength that comes of harmonious action between equals; in the place of rounded arches, pointed ones, to show that the forces that conspired to raise the structure did not sacrifice their several individualities, but freely contributed each its share toward the attainment of the end; in place of squat, close towers', tall spires aspiring" to infinitude, and open on all sides, as much as to say, "Here we stand free and open, acknowledging no laws but those of heaven." Then came decoration of the window arches, which showed a different design in each, thus entering a protest against all stereotyped uniformity. This was the true Germanic or Gothic architecture, the triumph of the free Teutonic spirit, which favors the unhindered development and the unrestricted independence of individual genius. It was also the expression of mysticism, with innumerable spirelets striving heavenward to find the Divine. Hence the Gothic style has somewhat of gloom and melancholy in its vast arches and narrow windows. It invites the free spontaneous spirit of man to sound the depths of his own nature, and so is as adverse to obtrusive dogmatism as to reckless investigation, and illuminsm, which disturb prejudices. Hence as the Romanic style is the architecture of the popedom, so is the Gothic that of free church life; and then the architecture of illuminism followed as the style of the Renaissance.

2. The Stonemasons' Lodges of Germany

The meeting places of the masons' unions in the cities were the board huts that stood on the site of churches in process of construction, affording-shelter to the masons or stone cutters while at work. These huts, or "lodges," were at an early period leagued together, and the members of the leagues, in memory of their formerly having been inmates of monasteries, called one another Brother, and their unions Brotherhoods; they also bestowed on their chief officers such tokens of respect as are found in the clerical epithets "reverend" and "worshipful." The date of the formation of this league cannot be determined. It appears to have been in full swing in the 13th century, and the credit of its definitive organization is usually given to Albert the Great, Count of Bollstadt, a celebrated Dominican friar (b. 1200, d. 1280). Albert lived nearly all his life in Cologne, and therefore the famous Cathedral of Cologne is to be regarded as the cradle of the great league of stonemasons' lodges.

For the government of this league an assembly of delegates from the lodges, which came together "in chapter" (another reminiscence of the monastic origin of these unions) at Ratisbon in 1459, drew up a trade constitution entitled "Ordnung und Vereinigung der gemeinen Bruderschaft des Steinwerks und der Steinmetzen" (Regulation and Combination of the general brotherhood of stonework and stonemasons): it was revised and amended at Basel in 1497, and at Strasburg 1498. From this and other ancient documents relating to the organization of the brotherhood we gather that the Brethren were classed as Masters, "Parleyers" and Comrades (meister, parlirer, gesellen), and to these were added, though not as brethren, yet as dependents, Helpers, that is, apprentices. At the head of a lodge stood the Master of Works, or Master-Builder. The masters of the three lodges at Strasburg, Cologne and Vienna were the Chief Judges of the league, and he of Strasburg held the foremost rank among these. To the judicial district of Strasburg belonged the left bank of the Rhine down to the Moselle, and on the right bank Suabia, Franconia, Hesse; to the district of Cologne belonged the region on the other side of the Moselle; and to that of Vienna, Austria, Hungary, Italy. Switzerland stood apart under a separate master, who had his seat at Berne; Zurich afterward succeeded to the place of Berne. The masons of Northern Germany, on the right bank of the Rhine (Thuringia, Saxony, etc.), were only nominally members of the league: as matter of fact they were subordinate to none of these lodges, but they adopted a special "order" for themselves at Torgau in 1462. In these regulations we find many striking evidences of the sturdy good sense of the masons. For example, they were forbidden to disparage deceased masters and their works; also to teach others their art for money, for they ought to deal with each other as friends; one master was not to expel a fellowcraft; to do so he must not only take counsel with two other masters, but also a majority of the: fellowcrafts must approve; differences between masters should be settled by arbitrators chosen from members of the league.

In the brotherhoods brotherly comradeship played an important part. Meetings were held monthly, and the business ended with a feast. Each General lodge yearly held as grand assembly; and the festivals of Saint John the Baptist, and of the so-called "Four Crowned Ones," were holidays for the league. Each meeting of a lodge was opened and closed with questions and answers of the master and the comrades. To the journeyman, as soon as he began to travel, were communicated the secret signs of the brotherhood passwords, grip, etc. With these he identified himself as a brother mason wherever he went, and so had the right to learn the trade gratis. On coming to a hut where stone-cutting was going on, he first shut the door, so as to knock on it after the masonic fashion; then asked, "Are German masons at work here?" Forthwith the comrades made search through the hut, shut the doors, and ranged themselves in a right angle; the visitor placed his' feet at right angles, saying, "God bless the worthy masons;" to which the answer was "God thank the worthy masons," and so on, questions and answers many, among them these: "Who sent you forth"? "My honored master, honored sureties, and the whole honored masons' lodge at X." "What for?" "For discipline and right behavior," "What is discipline and right behavior?" "The usages of the craft and its customs."

Of the rites of initiation in those times we know nothing: what Fallou has on that head regarding the usages of the German stonemasons is simply borrowed from the Freemasons' ritual of the present time. It is highly probable that in the medieval masons' lodges the technical details of the craft and its secrets played the chief part in the ceremonies of initiation. The medieval stonemasons also employed as symbols of their craft the hammer, the circle, the square, etc., also mystic figures, e. g., the flaming star (which was the Pythagorean pentagram, or the magic hexagram two triangles laid across each other), the two pillars "of Solomon's temple, wine skins, ears of corn, interlaced cords, etc. The only other point of any consequence of which we have certainty is that the postulant swore to observe secrecy. But there is no doubt that the drinking usages as handed down to us are authentic. For example, the glass was never to be handed to the banqueter, but set on the table before him; then, he must not touch it save with the right hand covered with a white glove or a white napkin, when a special toast is drunk.

The masons' brotherhoods were. a distinctly Christian institution: the members were required by the "Ordinances" to comply with all the usages of the Church. This was a survival from the time when the lodges had their origin in monasteries. The sects that arose on every side despite bloody persecutions, and the illuminism spread abroad by them, contributed to bring about a change in the spirit of the masons which was noticeable in the 14th and 15th centuries: many, perhaps a majority, of them acquired a spirit of opposition to Roman ecclesiasicism, and it was very plainly manifested in their sculpture. More bitter satire cannot be imagined than they employed; and what is most significant is that it found expression in the churches themselves. Thus in a representation of the Last Judgment in the Berne minster a pope wearing a glittering tiara of gold is seen tumbling headlong into Hell; and in the vestibule the Wise and the Foolish Virgins are shown keeping vigil, but the foolish ones wear cardinals' hats, bishops' mitres and priests' caps. The Doberan Church in Mecklenburg shows a mill in which church dogmas are ground out. At Strasburg was seen a procession of all manner of beasts with blazing torches and an ass performing the mass; at Brandenburg was shown a fox preaching to a flock of geese, etc.

Illuminism is the foe of knighthood and ecclesiasticism, for illuminism knows no privilege of birth or of rank or of vocation. Hence, in so far as such bodies as the Templars and Stonemasons favored illuminism, they undermined the institutions to which they owed their existence, and so were working for their own extinction.

The downfall of the Stonemasons' brotherhood had its causes even in the age before the Reformation, in that there was no lack now of churches, and that hardly any new churches were erected. What the relation was of the lodges to the Reformation we shall see later on. The savageries of the 16th and 17th centuries, particularly the Thirty-Years' War, dealt a severe blow at the buildingcraft; but the deathblow to the Stonemasons' league was the treacherous seizure of the seat of the principal lodge, Strasburg, by Louis XIV. Naturally, the German princes interdicted communication of their subjects with foreign associations, and, of course, with the principal lodge in Strasburg, 1707. And as the discords of the German-masons and their weakness prevented them from instituting a new head lodge, the Emperor at one stroke did away with all lodges, principal and subordinate, and forbade the oath of secrecy, the use of the "nonsensical form of salutation" (so ran the text of the decree), and the distinction between "salutation-masons" and "lettermasons" (grussmaurer, briefmaurer). Nevertheless, the lodges remained as secret societies until modern freedom of industrial trades stripped them of all meaning, and cut the ground under their feet.

3. French Craftsmen

VERY DIFFERENT FROM the German societies of craftsmen were those of France. Whereas, in Germany we find strenuous endeavor toward perfection in the craft, cultivation of the beautiful, and a disposition no less elevated in a moral sense than devoutly religious; in France we see only rude, undirected effort, with here and there some encouraging features. In France there is sharp distinction between the gilds of the masters and the lodges of the journeymen. The masters have neither a common) bond of union, nor any common property; the craftsmen form strong societies, with secret constitutions and usages.

There are several societies of French craftsmen (compagnonnages), but they are not distinguished according to locality, but according to the supposed manner of their first institution and the branch of the craft which they represent. They are divided, first, into two great sections, the Compagnons du Devoir (companions of duty), and the Compagnons de la Liberte (companions of liberty). The former are again divided into the Enfants de Maitre Jacques (Master James's children), and the Enfants de Maitre Soubise (Master Soubise's children), but the latter commonly called themselves Enfants de Salomon. Between the Compagnons du Devoir and the Compagnons de la Liberte, as well as between the children of James and those of Soubise, there exists the bitterest enmity which is mirrored in their myths and traditions. According to the story of the Devoir comrades, at the building of Solomon's temple, Hiram, masterbuilder, to maintain discipline and order among the workmen, instituted societies with special passwords and secret ritual. But that act was the occasion of his death, for some workmen slew him because he refused to give them the countersign of the masters: those evildoers were the founders of the Compagnonnage de la Liberte! Now among the faithful workmen were two Gaulish masters, James, stonemason, and Soubise, carpenter: these, after the completion of the temple, returned home, and landing, one at Marseilles, the other at Bordeaux, founded societies after the pattern of those instituted by Hiram; and these societies, little by little, admitted craftsmen other than builders, but the two bodies lived in perpetual hatred of each other, each claiming priority. Each of them refers its own institution (on what grounds is unknown) to the years 558 B.C. and 550 B.C. respectively, and each possesses authentic documents in proof, though none has ever seen them. The Liberte tradition is the same as that of the Devoir, only the respective parts of the chief actors are reversed. In the bosom of La Liberte are gathered four crafts stonemasons, carpenters, joiners, locksmiths. The Devoir includes 28 crafts, and of these the children of Soubise comprise the carpenters, roofers and plasterers; to the children of James belong the stonemasons, joiners, locksmiths, and 22 other trades, introduced in later times, but all connected with housebuilding, except hatmakers. All other craftsmen whose work is the production of clothing and foodstuffs are excluded from the compagnonnages, and form separate societies of their own. The shoemakers and the bakers, in particular, are held in contempt, and persecuted in every way by the compagnons; while among James's children even the members of the building crafts despise their juniors (trades of less ancient lineage), and in their ignorance derive the word compagnon from "compas" (a pair of compasses), the symbol of the art of building; hence in tfeeir eyes the other trades are quite destitute of art or skill.

Even craftsmen of the same trade, but belonging to different leagues, whether Devoir or Liberte, oppose each other in every way. The carpenters of Paris have made an end of this strife by dividing the cosmopolitan city between themselves, the compagnons du Devoir taking the left and those of La Liberte the right bank of the Seme. With the other trades and in the provinces the case is worse, the hostile leagues, often engaging in street fights and pitched battles. Even in the same trade and in the same league hostilities often break out. Of the French corporations of craftsmen, those of the building trades, especially the stonemasons, probably arose about the same time as the German masons' lodges: at least there existed in the Middle Age in southern France, a society of bridge-builders, who, for the behoof of pilgrims to the Holy Land and wayfarers in general, maintained bridges, roads and inns. The earliest known charter was granted in 1189, by Pope Clement III., who, like his third predecessor, Lucius III., took them under his protection. As emblem they wore on the breast a pointed hammer. The other compagnonnages can show no authentic records of earlier date than the 14th century. The most ancient of them is the society of the Dyers, dating from 1330. Admission to* these societies involves many ceremonies derived from the ritual of the Catholic Church; hence, the Tailors and Shoemakers were in 1645 denounced to the ecclesiastical tribunals, and their meetings forbidden by the theological faculty of Paris.

4. The English Stonemasons

WHILE THE GERMAN societies of handicraftsmen were oppressed by the imperial power, and the French societies lived in obscurity, the English masons' lodges, on the contrary, attained high importance. Tradition traces English (operative) masonry back to King Alfred the Great (871-901), and his successor, Athelstan, whose younger son, Edwin, is said to have called meetings of masons, and to have given laws to their lodges. However that may be, it is certain that in England, as in Germany, important edifices were erected by the clergy, and that Dunstan, archbishop of Canterbury, was an accomplished architect; but after the rise of Gothic architecture the builders were laymen, and in all probability many of them Germans. In the early English societies of masons we find rules and usages that clearly follow German precedent, and the lists of master masons contain many decidedly German names. Nevertheless, English masonry showed some peculiar features, e. g., the station of the master in the east, the holding of the lodge meetings in open air in fair weather, the posting of guards around the lodge, the drenching of peepers with the drip from the roof "till the water ran out of their shoes," etc.

The English Freemasons may have got their name from the fact that the original founders of lodges were workers in freestone freestone masons, as distinguished from workers in rough stone; freestone mason, it is supposed, was afterward contracted to the form "freemason." In an act of parliament of the year 1350 the word freemason is found for the first time. By that act congregations and chapters of masons were forbidden. But the masons survived this persecution. Among themselves all masons were equals, comrades or fellows; in the lodges no distinction was made of master and fellow, though, of course, the actual master of a lodge presided over the meetings. The members studied mutual improvement in technical knowledge, and aided one another in misfortune. In the reign of Edward III. the laws prohibiting assemblage of masons was relaxed so as to permit meetings when held in presence of the sheriff of a county or the mayor of a city. Out of these societies of operative masons arose the modern institution of "speculative" freemasonry.

ASTROLOGERS AND ALCHEMISTS

THE EPOCH OF the Reformation closed with the recovery to the Catholic Church of a large proportion of its lost territory through the labors of the Jesuits. Long before the Thirty Years' War the zeal for religious creeds had died out; people had grown weary of theological strifes, though they had little taste for other serious matters; and thus it came about that in the transition from the 16th to the 17th century such pseudo-sciences as Alchemy and Astrology had great vogue. The study of Astrology had for its aim only fame and glory. and, therefore, was pursued openly; while Alchemy being inspired mainly by avarice, had its laboratories in dark cellars, and made a strict secret of its processes.

Hence, it was natural that Alchemy, or the pretended art of producing gold and silver, should give rise to secret associations, especially as it employed sundry mystic, theosophic, and kabbalistic means for attaining its ends, such as were used by the pupils and followers of the famous Theophrastus Bombastus Paracelsus, reformer of the medical art, and one of the most zealous of astronomers and alchemists. That was the era of a Jacob Boehme, shoemaker and philosopher, who, though he had none of the "accurst hunger" for the precious metals, gave an impetus to fatuous investigations of divine things.

At the beginning of the 17th century a multitude of writings about this mystic and superstitious business appeared, pro and contra. In this battle of goosequills the Lutheran theologian, John Valentine Andraea of Tuebingen (b. 1586, d. 1654), took a very prominent part. Andreae in 1614 conceived the thought of playing a trick on these mystics by publishing two satirical pieces, in which was given an account of an alleged secret society designed to promote studies of that kind; to this society he gave a name suggested by the design of his own family seal (a Saint Andrew's cross, with roses at the ends of its four arms) Rosicrucians. These writings, "Fama Fraternitatis Roseae Crucis" (Fame of the Brotherhood of the Rosy Cross) and "Confessio Fraternitatis" (Confession of Faith of the Brotherhood) traced the pretended society back to a monk named Christian Rosenkreuz, who, in the 14th and 15th centuries, visited the holy land, was instructed in the occult sciences in the East, founded among his fellow-monks the brotherhood called by his name, and died at the age of 106 years. After a lapse of 120 years, in his tomb, which, in accordance with the rule of the order, was kept secret, but which was a magnificent structure in a vault, was found resting on his incorrupt body a parchment book containing the constitution and the secrets of the order. A later document "Chymische Hochzeit Christiani Rosenkreuz" (alchymic nuptials of Christian Rosenkreuz), which appeared in 1616, span the story out to greater length. Now, so great was the alchemistic furore of that time that the tale passed for solemn' truth, and a swarm of writings followed, championing or battling against the Society of the Rosicrucians. To the opponents of the Rosy Cross belonged the theologians, who sniffed heretical tenets in the "documents," and the medical men who scented danger to their close gild; while the alchemists, and particularly the followers of Paracelsus, inquired diligently after the Rosicrucians, and maintained the authenticity of their Constitution. Nor was there lack of attempts at interpreting in a mystical sense the symbol of the Rosy Cross: it signified Holiness joined with Silentiousness; it typefied the rose-colored Blood of Christ poured out on the cross. Astounded by the war of no-wits against little-wits occasioned unintentionally by himself, Andreae tried to undo the mischief by putting forth two pieces, "Mythologia Christiana," and "Turris Babel, to prove that the whole thing was a joke, that the Brotherhood was a fiction and non-existent. But as he neglected to name himself as author of the first two writings, in vain did he pour out on the Rosicrucianistic partisans all the vitriol of his contempt. In vain, with a view to lead men's fancy in other directions, did he found a "Christian Brotherhood" for the purpose of purging religion of abuses and planting true piety. The insanity persisted. Alchemy, barely alluded to in Andreae's writings, became the subject of a multitude of new books, whose authors gave out that they were members of the alleged society. The incident was also turned to account by adventurers and by factions of every sort; the thing: went so far that in the Rhineland. and the Low Countries secret alchemistic societies were founded under the name of Rosicrucians, which also took the style Fraternitas Roris Cocti (Brotherhood of Boiled Dew), that is, of the Philosophers' Stone; but these societies had no general organization among themselves. Many a wight was choused out of his money by these schemers. There were branch societies in Germany and Italy. In England Dr. Robert Fludd, an ardent mystic and alchemist, propagated the singular order by publishing" a number of writings. With regard to the usages of the societies, we are told that the members roamed about meanly clad, with hair cropped close near the forehead, wearing as a token a black silken cord in the top buttonhole, carrying, when several went together, a small green banner. They claimed that their society was an offshoot of the great knightly order of St. John (Hospitalers). At their lodge meetings they wore a blue ribbon, on which was a gold cross inscribed with a rose, and their president (styled Imperator, emperor) was dressed in priestly togs. They observed strict secrecy as toward outsiders. They disappeared little by little in the i8th century, and there is no means of determining the relation between them and the masonic Rosicrucians, of whom more anon.

Rise and Constitution of Freemasonry

1. Rise of Freemasonry

THE REFORMATION AND the events connected with it had given people much matter of meditation. But the intolerance shown by the authorities and by the members of both creeds, in maltreating and persecuting their opponents, so alienated all humane minded men that secretly people began to care neither for the interest of Protestantism nor for that of Catholicism, and in the common brotherhood of mankind to disregard all differences of creed. Illuminism, which had been "good form" though in a frivolous sense among the Templars, and in a satiric sense among the Stonemasons, took a more dignified shape, not of incredulity but of earnest desire to build up, and to this consummation the English masons contributed materially. In England people had had enough of strife over creeds, enough of persecution of Protestants under "Bloody Mary" and of Catholics under the inflexible Elizabeth, and they longed for tolerance. They derived the principles of tolerance from renascent literature and art, which made such impression that as in an earlier age the Romanic architecture, so now the Gothic, as the expression of a definite phase of belief, lost its following, and the so-called Augustan or "Renaissance" style an imitation of the ancient Grecian and Roman styles won the day with all who knew anything of art. The Renaissance style was brought to England by the painter Inigo Jones, who had learned his art in Italy, and who, under James L, became in 1607 superintendent general of royal constructions, and at the same time president of the Freemasons, whose lodges he reformed. Instead of the yearly general meetings he instituted quarterly meetings: such masons as adhered to the manual craft and cared nothing, for intellectual aims were permitted to go back into the trade gilds; while, on the other hand, men of talent not belonging to the mason's trade, but who were interested in architecture and in the aspirations of the time, were taken into the lodges under the name of "accepted brethren." Under the altered circumstances a new, bold spirit awoke among the Freemasons, and it found support in the sentiment of brotherliness, irrespective of creeds, then everywhere prevalent This disposition of minds was promoted in an incalculable degree by the pictures drawn by Sir Thomas More in his "Utopia," and by Sir Francis Bacon in his "New Atlantis," of countries existing, indeed, only in their imagination, but which presented ideal conditions, such as enlightened minds might desire to realize upon this earth; also by the writings of the Bohemian preacher, Amos Komensky (latinized Comenius), who, during the Thirty Years' War was expelled from his country by the partisans of the Emperor, and came to England in 1641 writings that condemned all churchly bigotry and pleaded for cosmopolitanism. As men of the most diverse views, political and religious, were in the lodges, the order suffered severely during the civil commotions of the first and second revolution, but on the return of peace it more than recovered lost prestige. The rebuilding of London, and in particular St. Paul's Cathedral (1662), added greatly to the fame of English masonry: Sir Christopher Wren, builder of Saint Paul's, was of the brotherhood. But about the time of the death of William III. (1702), owing to slackness of occupation, in the building trades, the Freemason lodges became conscious of a serious defect in their organization. The members who were practically connected with the operative craft of masonry were steadily declining in number, and the "accepted" masons had become the majority. The lodges, therefore, had come to be ai sort of clubs, and this transformation spread rapidly in London.

Another influence that came in to affect the development of English freemasonry was the diffusion of deistical opinions by Locke's school in philosophy. Though the lodges then, as now, made loud protestations of orthodoxy, they could not withdraw themselves out of the deistical atmosphere of the period.

The resultant of these different influences gained the upper hand in the clubs or lodges of the quondam masons, now Freemasons. They now aimed at a more thorough betterment of morals on a conservatively deistical basis. But the necessity of a closer organization was recognized. Two theologians, Theophilus Desaguliers (who was both a naturalist and a mathematician) and James Anderson, together with George Payne, antiquary, were the foremost men of those who, in the year 1717, effected the union of the four lodges of masons in London in one Grand Lodge, and procured the election of a Grand Master and two Grand Wardens, thus instituting the Freemasons' Union as it exists at this day. What Jerusalem is to Jews and Mecca to Mohammedans, and Rome to Catholics, that London is to Freemasons.

Henceforth the masons of England were no longer a society of handicraftsmen, but an association of men of all orders and every vocation, as also of every creed, who met together on the broad basis of humanity, and recognized no standard of human worth other than morality, kindliness and love of truth. The new Freemasons retained the symbolism of the operative masons, their language and their ritual. No longer did they build houses and churches, but the spiritual temple of humanity; they used the square no more to measure right angles of blocks of stone, but for evening the inequalities of human character, nor the compass any more to describe circles on stone, but to trace a ring of brother-love around all mankind. It was, perhaps, a picture of the young league of the Freemasons that Toland drew in his "Socratic Society" (1720), which, however, he clothed in a vesture the reverse of Grecian. The symposia or brotherly feasts of this society, their give-and-take of questions and answers, their aversion to the rule of mere physical force, to compulsory religious belief, and to creed hatred, as well as their mild and tolerant disposition and their brotherly regard for one another, remind us strongly of the ways of the Freemasons.

Though differences of creed played no part in the new masonry, nevertheless the brethren held religion in high esteem, and were steadfast upholders of the only two articles of belief that never were invented by man, but which are borne in on the mind and heart of every man, the existence of God, to wit, and the soul's immortality. Accordingly every lodge was opened and closed with prayer to the

"Almighty Architect of the universe"; and in the lodge of mourning in memory of a deceased brother, this formula was used: "He has passed over into the eternal East" to that region whence light proceeds. Political parties, also, were not regarded among Freemasons: one principle alone was common to them all love of country, respect for law and order, desire for the common welfare.

Inasmuch as the league must prize unity, one of the first decrees of the Grand Lodge was one declaring illegitimate all lodges created without its sanction. Hence to this day no lodges are recognized as such which are not founded originally and mediately from London. Despite this restriction there sprung up even in the first years after the institution of the Grand Lodge a multitude of new lodges, which received authorization from the Grand Lodge. With these numerous accessions the need of general laws became pressing, and at request of the Grand Lodge, Anderson, one of the founders, undertook to compare the existing statutes of the order with the ancient records and usages of the, Stonemasons, and to compile them in one body of law. The result was the "Book of Constitutions," which is still the groundwork of Freemasonry. It has been printed repeatedly, and is accessible to everyone. Another foundation stone of Freemasonry was laid by the Grand Lodge in 1724, when it instituted the "committee for beneficence," thus giving play to one of the most admirable features of the order that of giving help to the needy and unfortunate, whether within the order or without.

The inner organization of the order, finally, was completed by the introduction of the Degrees. Brothers who had filled the post of Masters, on retiring from office, did not return to the grade of

Fellows, but constituted a new degree, that of Masters; on the other hand, newly admitted members were no longer forthwith Fellows, but only apprentices: these degrees were instituted probably in 1720; at that time no other higher degrees were known. The right to promote apprentices to the degree of Fellow, and Fellows to that of Master, previously a function of the Grand Lodge, was accorded to the subordinate lodges in 1725.

Soon Freemasonry spread abroad. Lodges arose in all civilized countries, founded by English masons or by foreigners who had received masonic initiation in England; these lodges, when sufficiently numerous, united under Grand Lodges. The Grand Lodge of Ireland was created in 1730, those of Scotland and of France in 1736, a provincial lodge of England at Hamburg in 1740, the Unity Lodge of Frankfort-on-the-Main in 1742, and in the same year a lodge at Vienna, the Grand Mother Lodge of the Three World-spheres at Berlin in 1744, etc. A lodge was instituted at Boston, Mass., in 1733, and front Boston the order spread to Philadelphia. Thus in the space of thirty years from its origin freemasonry existed in all civilized lands, and so did not lag behind its opposite pole, Jesuitism, in respect of rapidity of propagation. Opposite poles these two societies are, for each possesses precisely those qualities which the other lacks. The Jesuits are strongly centralized, the freemasons only confederated. Jesuits are controlled by one man's will, Freemasons are under majority rule. Jesuits bottom morality in expediency, Freemasons in regard for the wellbeing of mankind. Jesuits recognize only one creed, Freemasons hold in respect all honest convictions. Jesuits seek to break down personal independence, Freemasons to build it up.

2. Constitution of the Order

THE SOCIETY OF Freemasons, because of its historic propagation, through sets from the English stock and through further budding and branching of these, forms no unitary organic whole. It has no central or supreme authority, no common head, whether acknowledged or unacknowledged. Its sole unity consists in a common name and a common end, in the common recognition signs, in agreement as to the general internal polity, and in a general uniformity of usages, though these show marked differences also. But very different between one country and another are the methods employed for attaining the ends of Freemasonry; different also is the organization of the lodge and the arrangement of the work.

Regarding the common end and aim of Freemasonry there is lack of perfect definiteness. In this regard Freemasonry presents a strong contrast to its rival, Jesuitism, which has only too clear perception of its aim. But so much is absolutely indisputable, that the end of Freemasonry is neither religious nor political, but purely moral. "Freemasonry labors to promote the wellbeing of mankind": here all Freemasons are at one, though some of them may lay more stress on material wellbeing, some on purely moral, some on spiritual welfare, while again others will consider the wellbeing of the whole, and still others, the wellbeing of individuals as the object of the society. But as these several views are by no means mutually exclusive, but, in fact, complementary of one another, this lack of definition in the end of the society cannot be any hindrance to the' society's beneficent labors. And as matter of fact the society has wrought much good. Not only does it help its own members in need; no worthy person in need ever appeals to the order for relief in vain.

But as it is impossible that in so widely diffused a society the members should know one another personally, it became necessary to establish tokens by which a mason may be able to recognize the masonship and the degree of a fellow mason. These tokens consist of a word uttered in a peculiar, way, a sign made by various motions of the hand and a peculiar pressure given in shaking hands (the grip). The mason is also recognized by his knock on a door, his way of drinking, etc., provided he cares to make use of these methods of intimating his masonry.

Besides these peculiarities common to all Freemasons there! are specialties shared only by particular sections of the masonic body. The whole body of Freemasons, because of its diffusion among diverse nationalities, is divided into a number of "systems" differing one from another in the ceremonies of initiation, of promotion to higher degrees, of the lodge of sorrow, and of other occasions. The differences consist largely in the form and tenor of the solemn addresses and counter, addresses, or questions and answers with which the meetings are opened and closed: these forms are an imitation of the rituals of the ancient stonemason lodges, and of other secret organizations. The ritual for the reception of an applicant into the first degree, that of apprentice, is modeled on the stonemasons' ritual; and the ceremonies of the higher degrees are amplifications of the same originals, with embellishments. In brief, the ritual of admission is such as was used by the monkish and the knightly orders;

but the prototype of all these rituals was undoubtedly the ceremonial of baptism in the Catholic Church.

No doubt many persons are desirous of knowing what takes place on the admission of a would-be Freemason. For the sake of such persons it may be remarked that these ceremonies are different in different systems, and that consequently an exposition of them would require a more than ordinarily voluminous work; that, furthermore, when communicated in writing, they lose all the effect they have when employed in the act of initiation; and that they would be likely to make no impression whatever on one who should desire to know them out of mere curiosity.

In the ceremonial of Freemasonry symbols or emblematic devices hold a prominent place. Of these the most ancient are borrowed from the stonemasons' lodges, and, therefore, represent masons' tools and implements; other symbolic devices are reminiscent of various secret societies or of ecclesiastical rites. But both in symbolism and in ceremonial many abuses have, in the course of time, crept in, and innovations have been made which mar the native simplicity of the order and divert it from the pursuit of more useful ends.

The recognition signs, the ceremonial, and the symbols are the only secrets in Freemasonry. Mysteries, that is to say, knowledge of things that are hidden from all other persons, the order has none, and the claims that have been made in that regard are without foundation. Discretion, with respect to the business of the lodges and the membership, Freemasonry enjoins in common with many other societies; and so far the order is a close society, or a private society, and not a secret society. Of secret machinations and intrigues such as are hatched in the Jesuit order and in the secret political associations of our, time, there is no trace in Freemasonry.

The masonic organization of each country exists for itself and in entire independence of other countries. A minor union of Freemasons, consisting of members, all of whom, as a rule, attend its meetings, is called a Lodge. The place (city, town, village, etc.,) in which there arc one or more lodges is called Orient; the presiding officer of a lodge is the Master, and with him are associated two Wardens besides other officers. The assemblage of the members, as well as the place in which they meet, is called a lodge. A lodge may be an isolated one, that is, entirely independent; but that is rarely the case; as a rule each lodge belongs to a union of lodges, called Grand Lodge, or Grand Orient. The several lodges of such a union work sometimes on one common system, sometimes on different systems. Again, the grand lodges differ greatly in their organization. As a rule they have a Grand Master, with several Grand Officers, and these are either elected by delegates from all the associate lodges, or are named by certain specially privileged lodges. The freest masonic constitution, is that of Switzerland, adopted in 1844: there the seat of the Grand Lodge is changed in every five years. In monarchical countries the royal residence city is usually the seat of the Grand Lodge. There are in Germany eight grand lodges, whose jurisdictions overlap one another, so that often there may be in a given city several lodges belonging to as many different grand lodges: but that does no prejudice to fraternal harmony. France, Belgium, Spain, and Brazil have each two grand lodges, each with a distinct system of ritual. But in Holland, Switzerland, Denmark, Sweden, England,

Scotland, Ireland, Hungary, Italy, Portugal, and Greece all the lodges of each country belong to one grand lodge. In each of the states of the American Union there is a grand lodge, and the same is to be said of the larger states of Central and South America. In the British colonies and dependencies, India, the Cape, Australasia, etc., the lodges are under the jurisdiction of the Grand Lodge of the United Kingdom: British America, however, has its own Grand Lodge. The grand lodges of the world number more than 90, the subordinate lodges more than 15,000, and the members, perhaps one million, reckoning only those in good and regular standing; but this is only a rough estimate; precise figures are not obtainable in default of a unitary organization.

3. The Lodge

THE SEVERAL LODGES are named after persons, virtues, masonic emblems, historic events, etc. In America and England they are often designated by numbers indicative of the time of their foundation. A lodge may be erected wherever a certain number of resident accepted brethren, among them at least three masters, desire to effect an organization, and obtain the approval of the grand lodge having jurisdiction. An indispensable requisite for a lodge is a "well tiled" apartment one well protected against the intrusion of outsiders, spies, or eavesdroppers. Usually the lodge is a square oblong hall or room, furnished after the manner of the time and country, and decorated with the masonic insignia. The attire of the assembled brethren is usually black, with white gloves (emblematic of hands not soiled by unjust gain) and a short white leather apron, a memento of the stonemasons and of the obligation to labor. The use of other insignia and of tokens to indicate the rank of the officials is left to the discretion of the several lodges. In England and her colonies, in the United States, Belgium and France on festive occasions Freemasons appear in public and on the streets in full masonic regalia, bearing the emblematic insignia of the order: in Germany and Switzerland such parade is frowned upon by Freemasons as unbecoming.

A Freemason lodge is an Apprentice Lodge, a Fellowcraft Lodge, or a Masters' Lodge, according to the degree of its members. In the Apprentice lodge, masons of all degrees take part: its business is to deliberate upon the affairs of the lodge, and to admit new apprentices. In the Fellowcraft lodge the Fellows' and the Masters take part: its function is simply to promote members from the first to the second degree. The Masters' lodge is for masters exclusively: the masters direct the work of the apprentices and promote Fellowcrafts to the master's degree. Besides, in each degree there is given instruction upon the symbolism and work of the same this is called a "Lodge of Instruction." Each degree has its special meaning, a sum of doctrines and a certain number of symbols. The purport of the Apprentice degree is the seeing of the light in the spiritual sense the spiritual birth of man: an explanation is given of the nature of the order, its aims and its constitution. The Second degree deals' with the life of man, its joys, its griefs, its fears: teaches to withstand passion and temptation, to know oneself, and to form an idea of the model human career. Finally, the teaching of the master's degree treats of the end of life, death, its inevitableness; proposes for imitation the examples of great men who have given up their life for humanity; suggests thoughts concerning the immortal life. Sometimes, also, the three degrees are explained as the embodiment of the masonic motto: Beauty, Strength, and Wisdom. These degrees are also known as the Saint John degrees, and the lodges as lodges of St. John, the Baptist being the chosen patron of the order, as he was also of the medieval stonemasons and of the Templars. The fact that the masons are under the patronage of Saint John the Baptist is interpreted to mean that the order is the forerunner of a happier condition of mankind, as John was the forerunner of Jesus. On the feast of Saint John (June 24th) or thereabout, in the year 1717, the first meeting of the Grand Lodge of London was held; and on that same day there is held in every masonic lodge throughout the world a festival at once grave and joyful.*

All males who have attained legal majority, and who are of good repute and their own masters, are eligible for admission to the order, without regard to race, station, calling, or creed. Unfortunately, Freemasons have not always and everywhere been free from antiquated prejudices in the admission of new members. Down to this day lodges in the United States shlut their doors in the face of

---

* We make no mention here of the so-called "higher degrees," which are in fact but amateurish fabrications, without any practical aim. They are distasteful forms of the true freemasonry; they differ as to name and number between one system and another; and the true lodges of Saint John freemasons recognize no such "supergraduation." The higher degrees are considered in another part of this work.

men of color, i. e., of those who are not whites; and many German, Danish, and Swedish lodges, both grand and particular, exclude Jews; in consequence, there are very many lodges of colored men and in Germany some Jewish lodges, whereas in the British colonies brethren of all colors and creeds work together in the same lodges.

Women and children are not altogether shut out from Free-masonry everywhere. It is the almost universal custom to admit, before the attainment of majority, masons' sons, who may have been instructed by 'their fathers as to the meaning of Freemasonry. There are also special meetings which the wives, the betrothed, the sisters, and the daughters of masons are permitted to attend. But we have an unmasonic excrescence and an abuse when, as in French lodges, with doors open to the public, a masonic baptism and a mason-ic marriage ceremony are performed with special ritual; still more worthy of reprobation are the Adoption lodges or Women's lodges, instituted at various times in France: in these women were initiated with a ceremonial adapted to the occasion, and were promoted to various degrees; thus, before the Revolution the luckless Princess de Lamballe, in the time of Napoleon the Empress Josephine, and under the Restoration the Duchess de Larochefoucauld were presidents of lodges. In other quarters also the cry has been raised for the ad-mission of the fair sex: but needless to say that such an innovation would very seriously compromise the gravity, the dignity, and the secrecy of the order, and breed trouble, both in the lodges and in. the families of the members. Once a woman was unwittingly admitted to the secrets of Freemasonry. Elizabeth Aldworth, daughter of the Irish viscount Donneraile, in whose house a lodge used to hold its meetings, on one occasion, in her young girlhood, peeped through a crack in a partition and witnessed the admission of a mason. She was caught in the act, and, to prevent betrayal, was herself initiated. In her after life she was noted for her acts of benevolence, and once, wearing the masonic togs, headed a public walk of the brethren. The Empress Maria Theresa also, it is said, dressed in man's apparel, once stole into a ledge in Vienna, having been informed that her husband, the Emperor Francis, was in the habit of meeting women there; but as she saw no women in the lodge, she withdrew in haste. Quite recently a Hungarian lodge admitted to membership a countess resident in its locality; but the Grand Lodge of Hungary canceled the act.

Secret Societies of the Eighteenth Century

1. Miscellaneous Secret Societies

CONDITIONS IN THE 18th century were specially favorable to the vogue of secret organizations: illuminism was making headway, but at the same time there remained many a relic of medieval barbarism. The manifest contrasts of opinion naturally inclined men of like mind to come together in secret societies for the advancement of their favorite principles. These societies copied the methods of Freemasonry, and were, in a) greater or less degree its rivals. Some of them admitted women to membership.

The societies of both! sexes were intended to compensate women for their exclusion from the Freemason lodge. The "Order of Woodsplitters" (fendeurs), founded in 1747 by the Chevalier Beauhaine, a distinguished Freemason, took its symbolism entirely from the work of the woodsplitter or woodchopper; the lodges were yards (i. e., woodyards, chantiers), the members were cousins (cousins, cousines; i. e., male and female cousins), the candidate was a Steel (used to strike fire from a flint), and so forth. The "Order of Hope" (esperance) was founded expressly for the behoof of Freemasons' wives, and they alone were admitted; but masons of the higher degrees could visit the lodges without initiation. The president was a woman. There were Esperance lodges in several cities of Germany; at Goettingen the university students joined the order for the sake of the refinement of manners got from association with the ladies. There is some doubt as to the true character of the "Order of Saint Jonathan" (afterward of Saint Joachim), qualified as "for True and Perfect Friendship," or "for the Defense of the Honor of Divine Providence." Its end would seem to have been to propagate belief in the Trinity, to refrain from the dance (especially the waltz), and from games of chance; also (this for the female members) to nurse their own children. It was founded by some German nobles, and its first grandmaster was Christian Francis, Duke of Saxe-Coburg. Though Protestants and Catholics were members of the order, it took on a strongly Catholic character, and in 1785 adopted the style of "the knightly Secular Chapter of the Order of Saint Joachim, the blessed Father of the Holy Virgin Mary, Mother of Our Lord and Savior Jesus Christ" (ritterlich-weltliches ordenskapitel von St. Joachim, etc.) The society passed quietly out of existence. The "Order of the Pilgrims' Chain" (Kette der Pilgrime), in Germany and Denmark, whose members belonged to the higher classes, had for its motto "Courtesy, Steadfastness, and Silence" (Willfaehrigkeit, Bestaendigkeit, Stillschweigen), and wore in a buttonhole a white ribbon bearing the initial letters of those three words. The members, male and female, were called Favorites (Favoriten); to admit a new member was "to add a link to the chain"; and any member could add any "link" whom he might have known for half a year. The symbolism was borrowed from travel. The "Order of Argonauts" was founded in 1772 by Conrad von Rhetz, a Brunswick Freemason. On an islet in a pond leased to him by the state, he built a temple in which the members were initiated. They approached the temple in barges and there were entertained by the Grand Admiral, as the founder was styled. There was no fee for admission. The motto was "Long Live Gladness"; the badge of the order was a green-enameled anchor of silver. The officers, besides the Grand Admiral, were the Pilot, the Ship's Chaplain, and so forth, and the members were Argonauts. After the founder's death the order went to wreck, and the temple disappeared, leaving no vestige. The renowned Fenelon founded at Douai an order called "the Palladium," its secret dialect was taken from his romance "Telemasque."

The "Order of the Mustardseed" said to have been founded in England in 1708: it spread over Holland and Germany: it assumed the form of a Protestant clericoknightly order, and concerned itself chiefly with religious affairs: its emblem was a gold cross, with mustard tree in the middle. This society was reputed to be connected with the Herrnhuters (Moravian brethren). The "Order of the Leal" (Order der Echten), founded in 1758, at Landeshut, by Bessel, a Prussian military officer, had for its end simply good-fellowship: it labored to win over to Prussia the Silesian nobility.

The "Society of the Ducats" (Dukatensocietat) had for its founder (1746) Count Louis of Neuwied, colonel in the Prussian Army. The members contributed one ducat a month; but when a member induced outsiders to join the society, then for the first outsider his own contribution for the month current was remitted; for the third, fifth and each following: odd-numbered new accession procured by him he received a ducat. This vulgar swindle, which was the sole end of the society, worked finely, and the membership grew rapidly: but the Society of the Ducats was suppressed by the government after an existence of two years.

Attempts to establish other fraudulent orders were made by a swindler who understood the foible of his contemporaries for mysteries. Matthew Grossinger, or as h styled himself, Francis Rudolf von Grossing, son of a butcher, born 1752 at Komorn in Hungary, would seem to have been once a Jesuit. After the suppression of his order, he offered to sell to Frederic the Great some Austrian official documents, but met with a repulse; then he represented himself to Joseph II. as a victim of the reactionary policy of the preceding reign, and in 1784 founded in the interest of his own pocket the "Order of the Rose," and again in 1788, 'donning women's clothes, the "Order of Harmony," both orders admitting members of either sex. He named "Frau von Rosenwald," a nonexistent personage, as head of the order, with the title Stiftsrose (The Institute's Rose). The several local societies were known as Roses, and their presiding officers as Rosylords and Rosyladies (Rosenherren, Rosendamen). But in fact Grossing was all in all, and he appropriated to himself the very liberal contributions and all other income: for that end alone were the societies established. He died in wretched circumstances, having always squandered his gains in luxury and extravagance.

2. Obscurantist Influences

THE DAYBREAK OF illuminism in the 18th century gave to the partisans of the ancient despotism of creed and privilege matter of most serious concern. They saw all their contrivances for keeping the people ignorant and submissive baffled. For them, as for the Papacy at the daybreak of the Reformation the question was, To be or Not to be. But theirs was a war with a far more redoubtable foe than Protestantism ever was. Illuminism did not aim merely at separation from the Roman Church: it declared a war of extermination against Rome, it aimed at abolition of all authority that presumed to determine the beliefs of men or to dictate their opinions. To down this hateful spirit of illuminism with one blow what satisfaction that would afford to the obscurantists of that time! But where should they begin? It was vain to think of silericing the literary champions of illuminism. The age of witch trials and courts of Inquisition was past. The problem was to find an organized institution in which the odious spirit of illuminism was, as it were, incorporated, and that could be no other than the society of the Freemasons. But the experience of the Popes and the Inquisition had shown that Freemasonry was not to be overmastered by persecution, by prisons, or by the stake. Hence, other champions must take the place of the Dominican inquisitors: the Freemasons must be won over to the good cause by flatteries and cajoleries. Among the illuminists of that day the Jesuits were regarded as the agents chosen for carrying out this plan; and though it cannot be demonstrated that they had an actual part in the business, the scheme surely was one quite consonant with the spirit of their order. The plan was shrewdly contrived. It dealt with political considerations affecting England, the native home of free-masonry; and thus the conspiracy aimed, so to speak, at capturing the den of the "dragon" of illuminism. The Stuart dynasty, which had returned to the Catholic fold, was in exile from the end of the 17th century, but, aided by France materially and by Rome intellectually, was ever striving to regain the lost throne. The efforts of kings and kings' sons in exile possess a poetical and romantic quality. It was possible to win over all sympathetic enthusiasts by exploiting their foibles, the nobles and legitimists (the Tories) by preaching legitima-cy, and the whole body of the Catholics by appealing to their loyalty to the Church. Now, the masonic order was a secret society, and as such, of course, was a rallying point for all enthusiasts, mystics, and dreamers. Besides, the nobility was strongly represented in the society: after the first four grandmasters of the Grand Lodge of Eng-land, who were all practical masons (architects), all the succeeding grandmasters belonged to the highest nobility of the realm. Among them we find dukes of Montague, Richmond, Norfolk, Chandos, to say nothing of a long series of viscounts, earls, and marquises. As for the Catholic element, it had many things in common with Free-masonry ceremonies and mysticism, hierarchic degrees, arid cosmo-politan extension; hence, with a little Jesuit finesse, the order might gradually and insensibly be made Catholic, as had been done with the Buddhist ceremonial in India: in this way the Society of Saint John might be transformed into a preparatory school for the Society of Jesus. And now, if we consider what a scandal it must have been to the coronetted chiefs of Fremasonry that their order originated among mechanics, we can see how easy it would be, by dishing up a few fables in proof of a nobler origin, to make converts of them for any ends whatever. In the event of success, the stronghold of illuminism would be captured, and with the help of its former champions the most powerful kingdom in Europe, and a great centre of illuminism, would be given back to a Catholic King, and thereby the road to conquest opened for the Church of Rome. Of course, these vast designs could not be carried out all at once. The work had to proceed by stages, as thus:

1. Aristocratic sentiment would be gratified by the institution of higher masonic degrees;

2. These degrees would be connected with the religious orders of knighthood by a chain of fable;

3. Obstinate Protestants would be quieted by the offer of a cryptic Catholicism which apparently would be in accordance with their own beliefs;

4. Persons inaccessible to religious considerations would be influenced by hopes of riches to be acquired through the secret arts of alchemy, and the like;

5. The whole purpose of the order would be directed toward spiritual and Catholic ends; finally,

6. when the process was completed, there would stand forth in all its nakedness the savage fury of the Inquisition.

3. The "High Degrees" Swindle

WITHOUT ANY SUFFICIENT reason assigned, there arose in England between the years 1741 and 1743 a new degree, Royal Arch, at first as a higher division of the master's degree afterward as an independent degree. Its content was a hotchpotch of New Testament passages, religious dogmas, and masonic, or, rather, unmasonic fables. Its tradition went back to the building of the second Temple of Jerusalem, after the return from Babylonian captivity; hence the president of a Royal Arch lodge took the name of Zerubbabel, and wore a vesture of scarlet and purple. The meeting was called a "chapter"; the three masonic degrees were dubbed "probationary degrees"; and soon, on the title page of the rules of the degree was represented an ark, with the inscription "Nulla Salus Extra" (no safety outside), whereby we are reminded that according to Catholic doctrine the ark of Noah was a type of the Church. Afterward the Royal Arch degree published a program of its work, in which masonry is divided into Operative and Speculative, and the former subdivided into manual, instrumental, and scientific; the aim of the "order" was defined to be, to gather the human race in one fold under the great Shepherd of souls. For the rest, the work of this degree was childish play.

Even before this fruit was born in England, there came into circulation in France, how or why nobody knows, a statement that Freemasonry arose in Palestine during the Crusades, and was there consolidated with the Knights of St. John (Hospitalers), wherefore the lodges came to be called Sai'nt John's lodges; that after the Crusades

the order was established in Scotland, was thence afterward introduced into England, and later into other countries. This historic lie
was, of course, welcomed by the nobles who were members of the
order; as for the many uneducated members who had been admitted
into the French lodges, they were easily deluded. Thenceforward
there were High Degrees of all sorts in France. And as the fable
assigned to Scotland the foremost place in the history of masonry,
the highest degrees began to be known as Scottish, or, after the
name of Scotland's patron, Saint Andrew, Saint Andrew's degrees,
and the lodges Scottish or Saint Andrew's lodges. In their rites of
admission they adopted from the traditions of the English and French
stonemasons a lot of myths about the death of Hiram, and taught the
aspirants for admission to avenge that death, the meaning being that
they were to avenge the expulsion of the Stuarts, and the wrongs
done the Catholic Church by the Reformation and by illuminism.

But as degrees were multiplied the Hiram myth no longer suf-
ficed, and for the higher steps it was necessary to have recourse to
other myths. Meanwhile it was seen that the story of the consolidation of the Freemasons and the Knights of Saint John would not
work, for that knightly order was still in existence; therefore, if the
aristocratic brethren were to have their vanity flattered, recourse
must be had to a suppressed order of knighthood. True, that was not
pleasing to strict Catholics, but there was no alternative and a bond
of connection had to be formed between Masonry and the order of
the Templars the heretical Templars.

So here is the story of the relation of the Freemasons to the
Templars: A few Templars, fleeing from papal and royal persecution

among them Grand Comptroller Harris and Marshal Aumont reached Scotland, and in that country, in order to gain a livelihood, worked as common masons. Advised of the death of the Grandmaster Molay, and of his last will, wherein he had directed the brethren to perpetuate the order, these fugitive knights that same year established the "Fremasons' league, and on the Scotch Isle of Mull held the first "chapter" in 1314. Now, to say nothing of the fact that, as we shall see, the story took more than one different shape! afterward, it is on other grounds quite unworthy of belief. It is beyond question that documentarily the Freemason league can assign for itself no other origin but the constitution of the Grand Lodge of England in 1717. But, besides, the story is ridiculous, not only in that Harris and Aumont are purely fictitious personages, but also in that the Grand Lodge of Scotland and the oldest lodges of that ancient kingdom know nothing of any such creation of a society; and, furthermore, the objects and the sentiments of Templarism and masonry differ too widely for any unification to take place between them. In the one body free thinking through levity of temperament: in the other repudiation of odium theologicum out of love of fellowmen; on one side egotism: on the other regard for the general weal; on one side pride of aristocracy: on the other regard only for the dignity of manhood.

And yet the most eminent men of the 18th century were fooled into believing that the Freemasons are descended from the Templars. The first serious and formal introduction of spurious Templarism into masonry took place in France. The Chevalier de Boneville, on November 24, 1764, founded at Paris a chapter of the high degrees called (apparently in honor of the then grandmaster of Freemasons, Louis de Bourbon, count of Clermont) the "Clermont chapter"; its members were, for the most part, partisans of the Stuarts, and therefore of the Jesuits also. Here it was that the story of the wondrous transformation of Templars into Freemasons in Scotland was invented, taught, and employed as part of the ceremonial of admission to the higher degrees. The members wore the masonic togs, and in their ritual the death of the Grandmaster Molay took the place of that of Hiram; and, in fact, by Hiram, as some asserted, Molay was meant. From this chapter the influence of the Jesuits extended soon over the whole field of French Freemasonry. Surely, it was not by accident nor out of patriotism that the very next year the French Grand Lodge, till then dependent on England, declared itself independent, and adopted statutes according to which thJe "Scottish Masters" (unknown both in England and Scotland) were to have oversight of the work.

4. Apostles of Nonsense

SOON THE CRAZE spread further still, and, first, of course, through Germany, where, in those degenerate days, whatever bore the French stamp was received with reverence and conscientiously aped. The Scottish lodges got entrance into Berlin as early as 1742. The dubious honor of this importation belongs to Baron E. G. von Marschall, who had been initiated into the new Templarism at Paris.

Dying soon afterward, he was succeeded by a man who presented the curious spectacle of noblest and most strenuous endeavor toward a fantastic goal, of the nature of which he knew nothing. Charles Gotthilf, Imperial Baron of Hund and Altengrottkau (so he was styled), born in 1722, was a nobleman of Lusatia and actual privy councilor of the Emperor; he was ai man of narrow mind, without high education, but he was an idealist, a chivalrous, hospitable and kindly gentleman. At Paris he was received into the Catholic Church and into the spurious order of Templars, to which he was devoted heart and soul: he was commissioned "Master of the Host" in Germany. He founded a lodge on one of his estates, which bore the ominous name of Unwurde (unworth), and soon had several subordinate lodges under his jurisdiction.

"About this time," says a contemporary writer, "the Seven-Years War broke out. The French troops came into Germany, and with them many Jesuits. With the French Army, and particularly in its commissariat, were a great many Freemasons of the higher degrees, and some of those gentlemen had calculated to make a good deal of money by the sale of merchandise in Germany. I knew one French commissary who had a whole wagonload of decorations for some forty-five degrees, and these he peddled all the way from Strasburg to Hamburg. Thereafter no German lodge was any longer content with the three symbolic degrees, but nearly every one of them had a series of higher degrees of one brand or another, according to the particular windbag each fell victim to; and so they dropped one system and took up another when a new apostle came that way and reformed them."

Such an apostle of fraud was the Marquis de Lernais or Lerney. Taken prisoner of war to Berlin, he there made known the Jesuitical doctrine of the Chapter of Clermont, and even founded a chapter in the Grand Lodge of the Three World-Spheres. To spread these chapters over the rest of Germany, or, in plain terms, to give the whole country into the hands of the Jesuits, a character by no means ambiguous, one Philip Samuel Rosa, once a Protestant clergyman, counsel to the consistory, and superintendent, but afterward deposed for immorality, was employed. Rosa's whole endeavor was to make money. Joining the Chapter of Clermont he got the title "Knight of Jerusalem and Prior of the Chapter of Halle." As he traveled up and down the land, the lodge at Halle paid his expenses. The eyes of the deluded brethren were at last opened, on the discovery of the relations between Rosa and another swindler, one Leuchte, who palmed himself off as an Englishman, Baron Johnson, and who founded a Grand Chapter, admitted novices and knights, boasted of armies and fleets at his command, and sent forth to all Templars in Germany an encyclical letter summoning them to his standard. Many were his dupes, among them Rosa, who visited him at Jena, humbled himself before him, and consented to the expulsion of the Berlin chapter from the "order." But as Rosa was loth to admit at Halle his submission to Johnson, and counseled the "knights" there not to recognize Johnson, his double-dealing was betrayed to his dupes at Halle by the "Baron," and he was dismissed from their service in disgrace. The "Baron" himself, after the discovery of his frauds, was repudiated by his followers, and in 1765 was imprisoned in the famous castle of Wartburg, and there remained till his death in 1775.

This was the opportunity of the Baron von Hund, the Don Quixote of the i8th century. He became now the acknowledged head of the "order," and ruled it as his fancy dictated. He always spoke of "Unknown Superiors" of the order as though his policy was guided by them; but the "Superiors" who imposed on the guileless gentleman were the intriguants at Paris. Because of the unconditional obedience required of the members, Hund called the system of the order that of "Strict Observance," in contradistinction to the "lax observance" of ordinary Freemasons. The Strict Observance comprised seven, degrees; viz., the three masonic degrees, the degree of the Scottish, Master, that of the Novice, that of the Knight-Templar, finally the degree of the Eques Professus, or Professed Knight (one who has "professed" or taken the monastic vows!). All knights assumed Latin names or surnames. Hund was Eques ab Ense (knight of the sword); others were Knight of the Sun, of the Lion, of the Star, even of the Whale, of the Chafer, of the Golden Crab, of the Mole, etc. Soon Strict Observance was dominant in the German lodges, while genuine Freemasonry was forgotten. No less than twenty-six German princes joined the order, and so puffed up were its directors in consequence that forthwith they divided Europe up into provinces, after the manner of the Templars and the Jesuits, naming for each province a Master of the Host. The subdivisions of provinces were called, as among the Templars, Priories, Prefectures, Comptroller-ships, etc. To give these subdivisions something more than an existence on paper, Hund dispatched the Baron G. A. von Weiler, Knight of the Golden Ear (of wheat, barly, etc.) to France and Italy, where he founded several chapters: even the Grand Orient of France united itself with the Strict Observance. Toward those German lodges which held aloof from this bastard masonry the Hundian Templars were supremely disdainful, and but few of the lodges had the spirit to speak out against the "obscurantist innovations." Chief among the few was the gallant old Lodge of Unity, at Frankfort on the Main, which declared itself an English provincial lodge, to show its independence of pseudo-Templarism.

A zealous apostle of the Strict Observance was John Christian Schubart of Kleefeld, Knight of the Ostrich, who was constantly on the road converting lodges to that system. Schubart devised a plan by which the order was to acquire great wealth. Hund's financial affairs were in confusion, in consequence of the war, and he proposed to bequeath his property to the order, in consideration of a certain sum in cash: but the order had not the money. Schubart now proposed to exact enormous fees for initiations and admissions to high degrees (for example, 350 thalers for admission). But the scheme could not be worked, and Schubart withdrew from the order.

The order had no longer any use for Hund. The time had come for the Jesuit influence to assert itself: it would have no more fooleries with helmets, swords, accoutrements, and Templar's mantles. It was seen by the original projectors of the "order" that if they would succeed in their design of winning over Freemasonry to the plan of catholizing Germany, they must betimes provide a clerical directorate for the organization, which till now had worn the mask of knighthood. They found a convenient instrument in the person of the Protestant theologian, John Augustus von Stark, born at Schwerin in 1741. While a student in Goettingen Stark was admitted (1761) to the masonic order; then he was a teacher in Petersburg, where he adopted the mystic system of one Melesino, a Greek. The ceremonial of Melsino's system comprised a number of prayers and genuflections, and even a mass; the high-degree meetings were called Conclaves, and the members wore surplices. Later, at Paris, Stark took an interest in Oriental manuscripts, and joined the Catholic Church, but all the same, on his return home he served as professor of theology at Koenigsberg, and then as court preacher and general ecclesiastical superintendent in the same city, and afterward in Darmstadt. Through some acquaintances, who were members of the Strict Observance, he got an introduction to Hund, to whom he revealed the great secret which he had learned at Petersburg, namely, that the grand mysteries of the Templars were revealed not to the knights, but only to the clerical members, and that these mysteries had been kept and handed down to that time; further, that the true chief of the order of Templars was none other but the Knight of the Golden Sun, Charles Edward Stuart, the Pretender, then resident in Florence. Delighted at the prospect of an enhancement of what he fancied to be his sciences, Hund recognized Stark and two of Stark's friends as Clerics of the Order of Templars. These clerical Templars thereupon drew up a ceremonial and created degrees of their own, and as a special favor initiated some secular knights into their mysteries. But because Hund declined to accommodate Stark with a loan of two hundred thalers to defray the expenses of a journey to Petersburg, where Pylades, head of the Templar clerics, resided, the two fell out, and Stark announced his purpose to keep the "Clericate" independent of the "Order." Nevertheless, he begged a friend to negotiate on his behalf with the secular Templars. This friend was a noble personage, Ernest Werner von Raven, Knight of the Pearl, a wealthy landowner, "prior" in the "order," member of a Chapter under Rosa and Hund, and also an initiate in Stork's own clerical order of Templars. Like Hund, he was a man of honor, but vain and narrow-minded, a mystic and an alchemist. Raven, in 1772, attended a convention held at Kohlo, in Lusatia, for the purpose of bringing about an understanding between the Knights and the clerics. He appeared in the costume of the Templar clerics, viz.; white cassock with red cross on the breast and a hat like that of a cardinal. He presented to the meeting a project of union drawn up by Stark, which the knights received with! plaudits of satisfaction. Hund was deposed from his high office, and appointed one of the Masters of the Host, while Duke Ferdinand of Brunswick was made Grandmaster, and other princes were named to be Superiors! and Protectors under him.

But the ritualistic pomp of the Clerics had already awakened suspicion in the minds of the Protestant members, and they began to cry out against mysteries of foreign origin and against the dictation of unknown Superiors. This discontent found expression in the convention held at Brunswick in 1775. There Hund was questioned as to the legitimacy of his appointment as a Master of the Host and the Clerics as to the authenticity of their mysteries. Hund was deposed from office; the following year he died of a broken heart, and, clothed in the regalia of Master of the Host, was interred in the church at Melrichsstadt in front of the altar. The seat of the Grandmaster was fixed permanently at Brunswick.

Thus the machinations of the Jesuits seemed to have come to naught. But now they sent forth a new apostle, a man who was an enigma, whose place of birth and of death are unknown, and who himself admitted to his confidants that he was an agent of the Jesuits. Gugomos such was his name styled baron and professor of art, and as a member of the Strict Observance Knight of the Triumphant Swan, in 1776, in his capacity as dignitary of the order of Templars with a long string of titles, invited the Grandmaster, the Directorate, and the Prior of the Clerics to attend a convention at Wiesbaden, in order, as he said, to instruct them in the genuine Templarism. And many "Knights" obeyed this singular invitation, among them several princes. Gugomos made loud boasts of the great number of mysteries into which he had been initiated, and in telling of them used phrases and terms that remind us strongly of the "Exercitia Spiritualia;" he exhibited his insignia and the commission of a "Most Holy See" in Cyprus; and declared that the Order to which he belonged, and of which the ancient order of Templars was only an offshoot, was founded by Moses, whose successors in the office of Grandmaster had been Egyptian, Judean, and other kings, Grecian philosophers, Christ himself and his apostles, finally popes. The Templar succession, he said, had been perpetuated in Cyprus (not in Scotland, then), and the archbishops of Cyprus were the successors of the Grandmasters. The degrees of Freemasonry (thus he driveled on) were a later innovation on the original clerical and knightly system, which in its organization was, he said, exactly the same as the Jesuit order. The one thing needed in order to instruct men in the occult sciences was a holy temple. On the completion of such a temple the "natural fire" would fall from heaven, etc. Many persons recognized the fraud; others walked into the trap, and were initiated. But seeing how little confidence was placed in him, Gugomos absconded, and that was the end of Jesuit Freemasonry.

But the farce of Templarism lived a few years yet, though people were growing tired of it. Some of the members went back to the old-fashioned masonry; others turned to new lights of mysticism that had for some time been looming on the horizon the Swedish Rite and the New Rosicrucianism.

5. The Swedish Rite

SWEDISH FREEMASONS, AS early as the middle of the 18th century, had found the genuine English masonry toe simple and inornate: they longed for more glitter and pomp, mysteries and degrees. King Gustavus III. attempted to satisfy this want by concocting a new system, the ingredients being genuine freemasonry, the Strict Observance, and the system then known as "Rosicrucianism," and in largest proportion the Clermont system: the doctrines of the famous mystic and seer, Swedenborg, may also have given a flavor to the compound. In founding the Swedish Rite or System, Gustavus counted on obtaining the help of the members in his effort to rid himself of the party of the nobles. The Swedish Rite has ten degrees. It is founded on two stories, one that certain secrets have descended to it from Christ through the Apostles, the clerical Templars, and the Freemasons; the other, that a nephew of the Grandmaster Beaulieu, a predecessor of Molay, visited Molay in prison, and, at the suggestion of Molay, went down into his uncle's sepulchre, where, in a casket, he found the insignia and the records of the order; that from Paris he took these into Scotland, and thence into Sweden. The symbols of the higher degrees refer to Templarism and Catholicism. The ceremonies of the highest degree are said closely to resemble the mass. Other alleged usages are, the wearing of the red cross of the Templars on the breast, reciting every night Saint Bernard's prayer to the Lamb of God, fasting on Good Friday till sundown, then eating three slices of bread, with oil and salt. The title of the head of the System is Vicar of Solomon. Several distinguished members of the Swedish System, among them the celebrated poet J. H. Voss, have characterized its ceremonies as "vain, useless and ridiculous."

6. The New Rosicrusians

THE NEW ROSICRUCIANISM had its rise in Southern Germany about the year 1760, while Rosa and Johnson were busy with their systems. Its originators had no connection with Freemasonry, and of its nine degrees not even the first three were named after the masonic degrees. Several discontented members of the Strict Observance joined the new order. The members assumed fanciful names, as Foebron,

Ormesus, Cedrinus; the lodges were called "Circles." Unquestioning obedience was to be rendered to the Superiors. The members learned only the mysteries of their own particular circle. The motto was: "May God and His Word be with us." They claimed to possess a cryptic Book containing a sacred history of events prior to the creation of the world, especially of the Fall of the Angels.

Their specialty was a mystical, kabbalistic, and totally absurd interpretation of the Bible, and of other alleged sacred or occult writings, whence they deduced an explanation of the universe. For example, they taught that the planets and the other heavenly bodies reflect back on the sun the light they receive from him, thus conserving his might and his splendor. They also practiced necromancy, exorcization, alchemy, the art of making gold, of preparing the elixir of life: they studied such problems as the production of the noble metals from rain water, urine, and other bodies, and even of evolving human beings by chemical processes. In their assemblies the members wore white and black scarfs, but those of the higher degrees wore priestly vestments, with crosses of silver or gold. At the initiation the candidates swore fearful oaths. Aspirants to the ninth degree were assured that once they should attain that eminence they would understand all nature's secrets and possess supreme control of angels, devils, and men. The first prophet of the New Rosicrucianism was John George Schrepfer, coffee-house keeper in Leipsic. In 1777 he founded in his own shop a lodge of the Scottish Rite, to afford his customers a better style of masonry than was found in the ordinary lodges. The Duke of Courland, protector of one of the masonic lodges, had the man publicly bastinadoed: but Schrepfer shortly afterward inspired both him and the Duke of Brunswick with a curiosity to be instructed in the mysteries, and visited them at Dresden and at Brunswick. In his lodge he gave demonstrations of his supernatural powers as a magician and a necromancer: for example, he would summon up spirits of the dead. Puffed up by success, Schrepfer indulged in all manner of debauchery, and at last" was reduced to penury. He died by his own hand, aged 35 years.

But Rosicrucianism was yet to reach its highest point, which it did in the person of John Christopher Woellner (born at Spandau, 1732, ordained preacher 1759, a councilor in the Prussian service in 1766, and Minister of State 1788; deceased 1800), and John Rudolf Bischofswerder. (born in Thuringia 1741, chamberlain to the Elector of Saxony; major in the Prussian army 1772; minister at war 1768; deceased 1803). Not content with the honor of being Knight of tHe Griffin in the Strict Observance, Bischofswerder went in search of an order that practiced the magic art, and was so fortunate as to find it in the New Rosicrucianism. He was initiated into the mysteries by Schrepfer, and it was he who converted the Duke of Courland from an enemy into a friend of the coffeehouse Rosicrucian. After the death of Schrepfer, whose most zealous supporter he had been, Bischofswerder obtained promotion in the Prussian service through the favor of the crown prince Frederic William, nephew of Frederic the Great, and shared his good fortune with Woellner. Knight of the Cube, who like himself had seceded from Templarism. The pair won the crown prince over to Rosicrucianism, and enjoyed his confidence both then and after his accession to the throne of Prussia in 1786, as William II. At last, as ministers of state, they succeeded in substituting obscurantism and state religionism in the place of the illuminism and toleration that had prevailed under old Fritz. It was they that dictated the odious Edict of Religion of 1788, which was expected to prove a deathblow to illuminism and free thought: but the death of the King upset all their calculations. That was the end of the New Rosicrucianism.

Simultaneously with the order of the Rosicrucians arose two variant forms of the same, the society of the Asiatic Brethren, anl that of the African Buildingmasters (Asiatische Brueder, Afrikanische Bauherren). The Asiatic Brethren's order was founded in Vienna by Baron Hans Henry von Eckhofen, an ex-Rosicrucian: it admitted only Freemasons, but did not exclude Jews, and its aims were the same as those of the Rosicrucians. Its chief seat was at Vienna, called by them Thessalonica, for they gave a foreign name to every place. Its head officers were styled Inquisitors. There were five degrees, viz., two probationary those of Seekers and of Sufferers and three superior degrees. The members in the two lower degrees wore round black hats with distinctive feathers for each degree, black mantles, and white or black ribbons, broidered with different emblems; those in the higher degrees wore red hats and mantles; the attire of those in the highest degree was all rosy-red. Ten members constituted a Mastership, ten masterships a Decade, and so on. The order became shockingly corrupt in Austria.

The African society, founded by War Councilor Koeppen in Berlin, had rather higher aims than the Rosicrucians and the Asiatic Brethren: they studied the history of Freemasonry, admitted to their order only scholars and artists, conducted their business in Latin, and of fered prizes for scientific researches: but they indulged in farfetched and absurd symbolism, kabbalism, magic, and mysticism. Their degrees were five inferior or preparatory, and five higher or esoteric. The order lived for a few years only.

There were many other societies, instituted mostly for the purpose of fraud and moneymaking: of these we give no account here. But there still remains one society which is worthy of mention that of the Brethren of the Cross (Kreuzbrueder) or Devotees of the Cross (Kreuzfromme), founded by Count Christian von Haugwitz (1752-1832), who was at one time Knight of the Holy Mount in the Strict Observance, afterward belonged to a German imitation of the Swedish rite, and at last founded a society which was described by a contemporary as "a conspiracy of despotism against liberty, of vice against virtue, of stupidity against talent, of darkness against enlightenment." The Devotees of the Cross observed the strictest secrecy, corresponded in cipher, inveigled princes, in order to rule ini their stead (after the manner of Bischofswerder and Woellner) and practiced all manner of superstitions to make an end of science. They had no connection whatever with Freemasonry.

Unfortunately this multiplication of mystical orders was not without effect on the fortunes of the masonic body, in that it has led to a vicious growth of "high degrees." It was a French adventurer, Stephen) Morin, who, in 1761, introduced into the United States the 33 degrees: they entered France again in 1803, and were regarded as a novelty, having been forgotten during the Revolution. The titles of these degrees are at once bombastic and unmeaning: Grand Scots, Knights of the East, High Princes of Jerusalem, Princes of Grace,

Grand Inquisitors, Princes of the Royal Secret, etc., and in some of the variations of these ridiculous degrees we have Knights of the Ape, and of the Lion, and Emperor of East and West.

The Illuminati and Their Era

1. The Illuminati

BY THE SUPPRESSION of the Jesuit order by Clement XIV., the results of two centuries of painful toil in the interest of a universal ecclesiastical dominion were undone. Then it was that an ingenious mind conceived the thought of employing on behalf of enlightenment such instrumentality as the Jesuits had employed against it. It was a pupil of the Jesuits to whom this thought first occurred: their mechanical, soul-stifling method of education had made him their enemy; but besides he had learned the artifices and the secrets of the Jesuits, and hoped that by imitating them in a Catholic country likely to be influenced by such arts, he might thereby promote the very opposite interests. Adam Weishaupt was born in 1748, and when only 25 years of age was professor of canon law and jurisprudence in the university of Ingolstadt, and also lecturer on history and philosophy, being the first in that institute to deliver lectures in the German language, and in consonance with the more enlightened spirit of the age. The intrigues of the ousted Fathers against their successor in a professorial chair which they had held for nearly a century forced to maturity the thought which he had cherished from his student days: and the founding in the neighboring village of Burghausen of a lodge of Rosicrucians, who were trying to attract to themselves his students, decided him to carry his idea into execution. On May l, 1776, he founded the Order of Perfectibilists to which he afterward gave the name Illuminists (Illuminati). To propagate this institution and to strengthen it he adopted measures which, in the circumstances of the time, seemed not unpractical. First, he adopted entire the hierarchic system of government existing among the Jesuits despotic rule from top to bottom; secondly, he employed Freemasonry to promote the ends of his order, just as the Jesuits had attempted to do. Accordingly Weishaupt, who was full of vanity, ambition, and desire of revenge, but knew nothing of the true Freemasonry, only of its perversions, obtained admission to the order in a lodge in Munich. Hence it is not true that the Freemasons founded the league of the Illuminati, but rather than, an order that arose outside of the lodge simply made use of Freemasonry: and so to the defeated reactionary movement against Freemasonry now succeeded an unmasonic revolutionary movement. In executing his plan Weishaupt was assisted mainly by Francis Xavier von Zwackh, of Landshut, councilor to the government of the Bavarian Palatinate, a man initiated in the highest degrees of masonry. Several years after its foundation the order of the Illuminati was still confined to South Germany, or even to Bavaria; but as Weishaupt desired that the north also, and Protestants no less than Catholics, should take an interest in his institute, he sent the Marquis Costanzo von Costanza, Bavarian chamberlain, to Frankfort-on-the-Main in 1779 to win over to the order the lodges in that city. Costanzo himself had little success, the rich merchants of Frankfort being averse to anything that would unsettle the peace of the world; but a young man whose acquaintance he made was destined to be, after Weishaupt, the most effective promoter of the new society. This was Baron Adolf von Knigge, well known for his much-read book. "Ueber den Umgang mit Memschen." He was born in 1752, and from his youth up had been an amateur of spiritism (ghostseership). He was already an Initiate of the higher degrees of the Strict Observance; but, dissatisfied with that order, he adopted the idea of Illuminism enthusiastically, and brought into the system a number of men who became its apostles; for example, Bode, the translator; Francis von Ditfurth, associate justice, of Weimar. With these two Knigge attended the Conventus of Wilhelmsbad, and there championed the cause of Illuminism stoutly, and helped to give the deathblow to Templarism. And now as Knigge, who supposed the order to be an ancient one, entered into a correspondence with Weishaupt, he was not a little astonished on learning from him that the society was as yet no more than an embryo: in fact, it had only the degree of the minor Illuminates (Kleine Illuminaten). Nothing disheartened, however, he journeyed to Bavaria, and was admitted to the order in splendid style. But his lively fancy led him to develop the order further; and the sober-minded Weishaupt, whose gifts were those of the thinker rather than of the contriver of forms, left to Knigge the elaboration of the several degree? and their Lessons, in which both were agreed that allusions to the fireworship and lightworship of the Persians should be employed, as typical of the spiritual fire and spiritual light of Illuminism.

The groundwork of thje polity of the Illuminati was as follows:

A supreme president ruled the whole, having next below him two officers, each of whom again had two others under him, and so on, so that the first could most conveniently govern all. The doings of the order were kept most strictly secret. Each member took the name of some historic or mythic personage of distinction: Weishaupt was Spartacus; Zwackh, Cato; Costanzo, Diomede; Knigge, Philo; Ditfurth, Minos; Nicolai, Lucian, and so on. Countries and cities also had pseudonyms: Munich was Athens; Frankfort, Edessa; Austria, Egypt; Franconia, Illyria, and so forth. In correspondence the members used a secret cipher, numbers taking the place of letters; in reckoning time they followed the calendar of the ancient Persians with the Persian names of months and the Persian aera.

The number of degrees'" and their designations were never definitely fixed, hence they are different in different localities. But all the accounts agree that there were three principal degrees. The first of these, the School of Plants (Pflanzschule) was designed to receive youths approaching adult age. The candidate for admission was at first a Novice, and, except the one who indoctrinated him, knew no member of die order. He was required, by submitting a detailed account of his life, with full particulars as to all his doings, and by keeping a journal, to prove himself a fit subject for admission, and one likely to be of service to the order. From the grade of Novice he passed to that of Minerval. The members of the Minerval class formed a sort of learned society, which occupied itself with answering questions in, the domain of morals. The Minervals, furthermore, were required to make known what they thought of the order, and what they expected of it, and they assumed the obligation of obedience. They were under the eye of their superior officers, read and wrote whatever superiors required of them, and spied on each other, and reported one another's faults to superiors as in the Jesuit system. The leaders of the Minervals were called Minor Illuminati; were taken by surprise at the meetings of their degree and nominated to that dignity a method that wonderfully stimulated ambition; they were instructed in the management and oversight of their subjects, and practiced themselves in that art; they were besides required to report their experiences. The second principal degree was Freemasonry, through the three original degrees of which and the two so-called Scottish degrees the Illuminati passed; and strenuous effort was made to have the masonic lodges adopt a system agreeable to the ideas of the Illuminati, so that the membership of the order might be steadily increased. The three original degrees of masonry were imparted to the regular Illuminati without ceremonies. The members of the two Scottish degrees were called Greater Illuminati, and the task of these was to study the characters of their fellowmembers; and Dirigent Illuminati, who presided over the several divisions of the illuministic masonry. The third and highest degree was that of the Mysteries, comprising the four stages of Priest, Regent, Magus and King (rex). This principal degree was elaborated only in part, and was not brought into use. In these four divisions of the third degree the ends of the order were, according to Knigge's plan, to be explained. The supreme heads of the! several divisions of the order were called Areopagites, but their functions were never fully defined. It was proposed also to add a department for women. The aims of this organization of the Illuminati remind us forcibly of those of the

Pythagorean League. They contemplated, not a sudden and violent but a gradual and peaceful revolution, in which the Illuminism of the 18th century should gain the victory. This revolution was to be effected by winning for the order all the considerable intellectual forces of the time, though the new associates were only little by little to learn what the aims of the order were. And inasmuch as , the members, when they should have among their number all those forces, must everywhere attain the highest places in government, the triumph of their enlightened principles could not be for long delayed. In the superior degrees the members were to be taught as a grand secret of the order that the means whereby the redemption oi mankind was one day to be accomplished was Secret Schools of Wisdom. These would lift man out of his fallen estate: these would, without violence, sweep Princes and National boundaries from the face of the earth, and constitute the human race one family, every housefather a priest and lord of his own, and Reason the one law-code of mankind. To imbue the minds of men with these principles, illuminist books were prescribed to the members for their reading. In sharp contrast to the masonic systems in which Jesuits had had a hand, the Illuminati avoided all forms which might suggest obedi-ence to any religion or church, and welcomed whatever favored the dominance of reason and the overthrow of revelation.

In the very short period of its existence the order of the Il-luminati attained a membership of 2,000, a result very materially promoted by the rule that any member possessing authority from the superiors could' admit a candidate. Among the members were many men eminent, both socially and in science, as the dukes of Saxe-

Gotha (Ernest), Brunswick (Ferdinand), of Saxe-Weimar (Charles Augustus, while yet only heir of the ducal crown); Dalberg, who was afterward prince-bishop; Montgilas, afterward minister of state; President Count Geinsheim; the celebrated philosopher Baader; Professors Semmer of lgolstadt, Moldenhauer of Kiel, Feder of Goettingen; the educator Leiuchsenring of Darmstadt; the Catholic cathedral prebendaries Schroeckenstein of Eichstadt and Schmelzer of Mayence; Haefelin, bishop of Munich; the authors Bahrdt, Biester, Gedike, Bode, Nicolai, etc. Goethe, Herder, and probably Pestalozzi also belonged to the order. The league in "Wilhelm Meister" reminds us strongly of the Illuminati.

The order was not yet spread abroad beyond the German borders, though a few Frenchmen had been admitted while visiting Germany; but its plans, were already reaching out farther. And now the head of the whole organization was to be the General (as among the Jesuits); under him there was to be in each country a head officer, the National; in each principal division of a country a Provincial; in subdivisions of provinces a Prefect, and so on.

This aping of Jesuit polity and the imprudent admission of objectionable or indifferent characters proved the ruin of the order. Despotic rule and espionage could never promote the cause of liberty and enlightenment and the founder of the order proposed to make enlightenment the means of attaining liberty.

Then the dissensions ever growing more serious between Weishaupt and Knigge. Whereas Weishaupt cared only for the ends of the society, all else being in his eyes only incidental, mere formalism, Knigge, on the other hand, being a man of the world, shrank in horror from the program of his associate: religion, morality, the State were imperiled. He dreaded Liberalist books, and would have been far better pleased to see the order working on the lines of the Freemasons of that day, though with an elaborate ceremonial and manifold degrees and mysteries, and with some harmless, innocent ideal of human welfare and brotherly love as the object of their endeavors. Weishaupt called Knigge's pet contrivance tinsel and trumpery and child's playthings, and the pair of "Areopagites" grew steadily ever more asunder.

This rising storm within boded less ill to the order than the attacks from without growing from day to day more violent. Illuminism was assailed by enemies of all sorts, that sprung up like mushrooms. First there were the masonic systems of the reactionary or superstitious kind, such as the Rosicrucians, the Asiatic Brethren, the African Masterbuilders, the Swedish Rite, the remnant of the Strict Observance, etc.; then such of the Illuminati as thought the hopes of the order had been disappointed, or who expected to profit by a betrayal of the order to the enemies of liberty and light; finally, and above all, there were the sons of Loyola, ever laboring industriously in the dark though their society had been suppressed, and now again, thanks to the licentious, bigoted despotic Elector Charles Theodore, possessing great influence in Bavaria, the country in which the membership of the Order of Illuminati was of longest standing and most numerous. At that court, the seat of corruption, some courtiers, professors, and clergymen who had been members of the order, with the secret pamphleteer, Joseph Utzschneider, at their head, played traitor, charging the order with rebellion, infidelity, and all manner of vices and crimes, and at the same time, "without ado, classing with the Illuminati the Freemasons. By a decree of August 2, 1784, the lodges of all secret societies established without government's approval, including the Illuminati and the Freemasons, were banned. The masonic lodges submitted at once, and closed their doors; but Weishaupt and his associates went on with their work, hoping to change the mind of the Elector by bringing up for public discussion their rules and their usages. Vain hope. The Elector's confessor, Father Frank, an ex-Jesuit, who already had labored against Free-masonry, procured on March 2., 1781, a second decree, by which the previous one was confirmed, and all secret organizations that continued to exist in violation of it, and specifically the Order of Illuminati, were forbidden to hold meetings, and all their property was confiscated. The Minister of State, Aloysius Xavier Kreitmayr, distinguished himself by the rigor with which he executed the ukaz. Weishaupt was deposed from his place at Ingolstadt, expelled from that city, and declared incapable of legal defense; he had to flee the country. He first tarried in Ratisbon; but soon, in consequence of the discovery of compromising documents in a search of the houses of Illuminati, very grave charges were brought against the members, and the Elector became alarmed for his throne. Without distinction of class or station a prosecution was entered against all persons accused of membership in the order, or even suspected of sympathy with it, and they were imprisoned, deposed from office, banished, and in the case of persons of the lower classes, pun-ished with stripes. This whole business was managed, without any recourse to" the regular tribunals, by a special commission under

Court direction. This persecution lasted till after the outbreak of the French" Revolution, and a refusal to condemn the French people was taken as evidence of a revolutionary spirit. This system naturally fostered ignorance among the lower classes, but among educated people it tended to spread the principles of Illuminism, and to awaken opposition to monkish rule in the state.

Weishaupt, no longer safe at Ratisbon, th Bavarian government having set a price on his head, fled to Gotha, where Duke Ernest, a member of the order, protected him, and made him Court councilor. Here he lived till 1830, but he failed to resuscitate his order on an improved plan. As for Knigge, he made haste to quit the incriminated order, and in his prim, emasculate "Umgang mit Menschen," strongly condemned all "secret societies" he, the old-time Templar, Freemason, and Illuminist. Few were so stout-hearted and firm as Ignatius von Born, the naturalist, a native of Transylvania, who had been a Jesuit, but who, after the suppression of the Society of Jesus, had joined the Illuminati and become a Freemason. After the suppression of the Bavarian lodges, Born, who was then in the service of the Emperor Joseph II. at Vienna, sent back to the Bavarian Academy of Sciences his diploma as member of that body, accompanying it with a letter in which he bluntly declared that he would rather be a Freemason than a member of a body with which he had nothing in common. And thus was the cry of Voltaire, "Ecrasons l'infame," taken up by the party against which it was first uttered, and by them given effect in the shape of a most infamous persecution, before men of enlightenment had made the first move toward "stamping out" what to them seemed an "infamy." For the rest it is said that the suppression of the Illuminati was the result of "an understanding with Frederic the Great, whose policy was threatened by the order.

2. Imitations of Illuminism

NOT LONG AFTER the break-up of the Order of Illuminati in the South, a similar order sprang up in Northern Germany. It originated in the brain of a man unfortunately at once a zealous Illuminist and a morally depraved vagabond, who made a deplorable misuse of the talents with which nature had endowed him richly. This was Dr. Charles Frederic Bahrdt, Protestant theologian, sometime preacher, professor, or teacher in sundry places, and once even keeper of an eating house at Halle. In 1788 it occurred to him to found an association to promote enlightened views, and his plan was to combine it with the masonic society, of which he had become a member in England. The projected association he called the "German Union of the XXII." (Deutsche Union der XXII), for the reason, as he explained in a circular letter, that twenty-two men had formed a union for the ends set forth. The Union was to be organized on the plan of Jesus Christ, whom Bahrdt in a voluminous work portrayed as the founder of a sort of Freemasonry, and of whose miracles he offered a rather forced natural explanation. In accordance with this plan the association was to be a "silent brotherhood" that was to hurl from their throne superstition and fanaticism, and this chiefly by the literary activity of the members. The literary labor was ingeniously organized in such fashion that the Union would by diligent effort in time gain control of the press and the whole book trade, thus acquiring the means of insuring the triumph of enlightenment. Outwardly the Union was to have the appearance of a purely literary association; but inwardly it was to consist of three degrees, of which the lower ones were to be simply reading societies, while the third alone would understand the real purpose of the order, viz., advancement of science, art, commerce, and religion, betterment of education, encouragement of men of talent, remuneration for services, provision for meritorious workers in age and misfortune, also for the widows and orphans of members. But inasmuch as Bahrdt had painted this beautiful picture solely to make money, the Deutsche Union existed only on paper; but it wrought for its projector a protracted term of imprisonment, which he survived but a short time; he died in 1792.

Another imitation of the Order of Illuminati, the League of the Evergetes (Bund der Evergeten, or benefactors, or welldoers) which sprang up at the close of the 18th century, had a longer term of life, though but little expansion. Its activity extended over all the arts and sciences, except positive theology and positive jurisprudence. The members were designated after the manner of the Illuminati; but they acknowledged no unknown superiors. Time was reckoned from the death of Socrates, B.C.. 400. The supreme head was called Archiepistat (archiepistates, chief overseer); there were two degrees, of which only the higher one had a political aim, popular representation. Fessler, by his protests against such tendencies, brought about a split in the association, and afterward his adversaries tried to convert it into a sort of moral Femgericht by tracking and branding all offenses. One of the three leaders betrayed the other two, and was with them put in prison, but soon afterward released: that ended the association.

3. Freemasonry and The French Revolution

THAT THERE WAS any alliance of the Freemasons, or even of the Illuminists, with the men of the French Revolution, which broke out in 1789, can be affirmed only by those who are ignorant of history or wilfully blind by men like the Privy Councilor Grolman of Giessen, friend of Stark (significantly named in the Strict Observance, Knight of the Golden Crab), or, like the abbe and canon Augustin Barruel in France, or the ship's captain and professor, John Robinson, in England: their allegations were received only with ridicule, and passed into oblivion. As we have seen, the Illuminati were to be found only in Germany, where no revolution took place: in fact, they were no longer in existence when the French revolution broke out. As for the Freemasons, we have already shown that they were opposed to the movement; but that movement could have no other ground than the dissatisfaction of the people of France with the shameful Bourbon dynasty, whose mischief could not be repaired by the well-intentioned but narrow-minded Louis XVI. No critical or serious work of history gives any justification of the belief that Freemasonry had a hand in bringing about that Revolution: but a decisive proof of the true relation of Freemasonry to the troubles of those times is had in the fact that the Terror made an end of the Grand Orient of France. All the clubs of the French Revolution were open: the people would not tolerate secret clubs, not even private assemblages, and hence as early as 1791 began to persecute the Freemasons as aristocrats. The Grandmaster then existing, Louis Philip Joseph, Duke of Orleans, gave up his title, as we know, and called himself Citizen Equality, and at last, in 1793, declared that he had given up the "phantom" of equality, found in Masonry, for the reality; that in the Republic there should be no Mysteries; and, therefore, he would no more have anything to do with Freemasonry. That same year his head fell under the guillotine, and his blood sealed the "reality of equality"; and most of the members of the two zealous lodges, those of the "Contrat Social" and of the "Noeuf Soeurs" were taught, when they met with a like fate, that "real" equality was a more dreadful "phantom'" than those they had pursued in the lodges. Only three lodges continued in existence through the Terror by extreme caution and secrecy, and not till the fall of the Terrorists did Brother Roettiers de Montaleau come forth from the prison in which he had been incarcerated simply because he was a Freemason.

Thus did French Masonry weather the terrible storm of the Revolution; the German lodges in the mean time were busy in reforming and strengthening themselves; for a season they withdrew into retirement, and exerted no longer any influence on public affairs. Superstition and child's play fell into disrepute: the Rosicrucians, the "Asian" and "African" orders, the Templars, and their like, condemned by public opinion, had to give up their absurdities and return to right reason. The general league of German Freemasons projected in 1790 by Bode of Gotha, failed of realization in consequence of the death soon afterward of that enlightened mason (1793); but its purpose was served, though not in its whole extent, by the sturdy Eclectic League of Masonry (Ekletische Freimaurerbund) founded as early as 1783, with headquarters at Frankfort. This League has ever since rendered notable service to the cause of genuine Freemasonry.

PART TWELFTH
Secret Societies of Various Kinds

1. Societies of Wits

THE COMIQ HAS a place everywhere in history: them is no lack of it in secret societies; indeed, in such societies it assumes many different forms. For there be secret societies that would be comic; there be secret societies that are comic without knowing it; and finally there be men and parties that by their action against so-called secret societies make themselves comic without intending it.

While Goethe lived at Weimar, there was formed in that city a satirical Society of Chevaliers. Curiously enough it was suggested by Frederic von Goue, a Knight of the Strict Observance and a strong believer in the descent of Freemasonry from Templarism, but a comical old soul withal, and author of a parody of Goethe's Werther. The members took knightly names: Goethe, for example, was Goetz von Berlichingen; they spoke in the style of chivalry, and they had four degrees. In sarcastic allusion to the revelations promised (but never communicated) in the high pseudomasonic degrees, the degrees of the Society of Chevaliers were, 1. Transition; 2. Transition's Transition; 3. Transition's Transition to Transition; 4. Transition's Transition to Transition of Transition. Only the initiated understood the profound meaning of the Degrees.

Another society of similar nature was that of the Mad Court Councilors founded at Frankfort-on-the-Main by the physician Ehrmann in 1809. Membership consisted only in the receipt from the founder (in recognition of some humorous piece) of a Diploma written in burlesque style in Latin, and bearing the impress of a broad seal. Among men honored with the diploma were Jean Paul, E. M. Arndt, Goethe, Iffland, Schlosser, Creuzer, Chladny, etc. Goethe earned his diploma by a parody of his own "Westoestlicher Diwan," "Occidentalischer Orientalismus."

Many societies of this sort have since arisen, but those of Vienna are worthy of special mention. One of these was called "Lud-lamshoehle," after a not very successful drama of Oehlenschlager's. It had many distinguished men in its membership. The members were called Bodies, the candidates Shadows. Though mirth was the only object, the police thought it best to suppress the society in 1826. In 1855 appeared the Green Island, a comic-chevalresque society, though it rendered good service to literature and art. Several writers and actors of note belonged to it. A society, the Allschlaraffia was founded at Prague in the 'fifties, which, in 1885, had eighty-five affiliated societies in Germany, Austria, Switzerland and other countries. A congress of the leagued societies met at Leipsic in 1876, and another at Prague in 1883. The president of each Schlaraffenreich (or society) was called Uhu, but on festive occasions was Aha, and in condemning offenses against the Allschlaraffia, Oho.

2. Imitations of Ancient Mystic Leagues

THERE HAVE BEEN and still are in France secret societies that have thought they could in our time transplant to Europe, under Masonic forms, the Egyptian: Mysteries. Once there was a Holy Order of the Sophisians, founded by French military officers who had been with Bonaparte in Egypt. The highest dignitaries were called Isiarchs, and the rest of the officers of the society bore similar titles (mostly fictitious) of Egyptian priests. The lodges were Pyramids, and their era began 15,000 years before Christ. Two orders which still subsist are those of Misraim and of Memphis, both of which in downright earnest trace their origin back to Egyptian antiquity and regard all the secret associations mentioned in the present volume, except those having political aims, as members of one grand association. The fact is that the Misraim system had its origin in 1805, and was founded by some men of loose morals, who contrived to get themselves received into a Freemasons' lodge in Milan, but who, because they were not promoted as they had hoped to be, went out and formed a Freemasonry of their own. The order spread first over Italy and in 1814 to France. The system has no fewer than ninety degrees, grouped in seventeen classes, and three series. Only the Grandmaster received the ninetieth degree: the "content" of all the degrees is pure nonsense. The Memphis system was introduced into France in 1814 by a Cairene adventurer. It held its first lodge at Montauban in 1815, but has often since that time been obliged to interrupt its work. The Grand Lodge of Paris was called Osiris, the head of the order was Grandmaster of Light; the hierarchy of officials was complex and showy. The degrees were more than ninety in number, to which were added three supreme degrees, but the total was afterward reduced to thirty. They comprised the Indian, Persian, Egyptian, Grecian, Scandinavian, and even the Mexican mythologies and theologies. Only two lodges exist today, and these the Grand Orient of France took under its wing some years ago, they having given up their silly ideas, and turned to sensible, beneficent work.

Another anachronism is the ghost of Templarism, which in the present century, as in the last, walks abroad: but its connection with Masonry is now rather loose, or even non-existent. Thus, there is no connection between Freemasonry and the New Templars of Paris, whose traditions do not differ from those of the New Observance. They reckon the years from the founding of the order of Templars (1118), and their "learned men" have imagined a succession of Grandmasters deriving from one Larnienius of Jerusalem, nominated, they say, by Molay as his successor. But Larmenius never existed. Here, then, is a new variant of the story put forth by the Strict Observance, the Royal Arch, etc. A document is shown to prove the nomination of Larmenius, but its Latin is not that of the 14th century; and, besides, only the Conventus of the Templars could name a Grandmaster. After the Revolution the new Templars purchased a splendid property in the Nouvelle France suburb of Paris, and from time to time observed the anniversary of Molay's death, having a solemn mass of requiem performed. The Grandmaster, Raimond Fabre de Palaprat (1804-1838) had under him four Grand Vicars for Europe, Asia, Africa and America indeed, the whole earth was parceled out among the members in Grand Priories, Minor Priories, Comptrol-leries, etc., and the wearers of these titles were happy. There were Clerical Templars, too, the highest grade being that of Bishop. The rules of the New Templarism permitted none to be admitted to the order save men of noble birth: but many a shopkeeper wore the white mantle with red cross.

There are New Templars also in England, Scotland, Ireland and the United States, almost all of whom have received the so-called higher degrees of Freemasonry. The English Templars are divided into two opposing parties, from one of which came the Irish and the American Templars. No one is competent for admission to any of these Templar societies who does not believe that Christ came on earth to save sinners with his blood, and the members must swear to defend this belief with' their swords and with their lives. But no one, alas, has yet heard of their deeds on behalf of those imperiled articles of faith. Their lodges are called Commanderies. They have Swordbearers, Bannerbearers, Prelates.

3. Imitations of Freemasonry

THE RESUSCITATION OF the ancient order of Druids is another ex-ample of imitation of the secret societies of antiquity. Among the Kelts of Gaul and Britain the Druids were, next after the nobles and the warriors, the highest estate. Religion, art, and science were their exclusive province: hence they were priests, poets, and scholars. Their head was a Chief Druid, and they formed an order with special garb, a special mode of writing, degrees and mysteries. The mysteries were certain theological, philosophical, medical, mathematical, etc., dogmata, and these were conveyed in three-membered sentences (triads). They believed in the immortality of the soul and its transmigration, in one god, creation of the world out of nothing, and its transformation (not destruction) by water and fire. Their assemblies were held in caverns and forests, on mountains, and within circles, ringed round with enormous blocks of stone. The Roman emperors persecuted them as they did Jews and Christians, because the Druidic mysteries seemed to them dangerous to the state. In Britain the Bards, i. e., those of the Druids who cultivated poetry and song, were the most influential division of their order. There were three degrees of the Bards Probationers, Passed Scholars and Learned Bards.

In 1781 a society was formed in London whose members called themselves Druids, and who practiced rites resembling those of Freemasonry. In 1858 there were twenty-seven mutually independent societies of Druids in Britain, but by consolidation the number is now reduced to fifteen. Druidism was introduced into the United States in 1833. Their local organizations are called Groves, and the central organizations Grand Groves. They have three degrees, to which are appended other higher degrees, each with its own High Arch Chapter. There is no close connection between British and American Druidism. In 1872 Druidism was imported into Germany from the United States: there are in the German empire forty Groves, with about 2,000 members. The order of Odd Fellows is of English origin, but is very strong in the United States. It was founded toward the end of the first half of the i8th century, but appears to have been at first a convivial society of "goodfellows," or odd fellows, with mutual benefit as a secondary object. It was reorganized in 1812, the feature of conviviality dropped, and the beneficent ends made paramount; this is the Independent Order of Odd Fellows. A rather similar organization, the Ancient Order of Foresters, was founded in England about the same time with the Odd Fellows' order. Forestry also has been transplanted to the United States. American Oddfellowship severed its connection with the British Grand Lodge in 1842. There were in the United States in 1889 more than 600,000 Oddfellows in 10,000 lodges. A society of American origin is that of the Knights of Pythias, founded in Washington in 1864; its object is to disseminate "the great principles of friendship, charity, and benevolence": it had in 1885 2,000 separate lodges and 160,000 members. The Order of Red Men (Improved Order of Red Men) is of earlier origin than the preceding: the members in their lodge meetings imitate some of the customs of the American aboriginals, and wear an attire resembling that of the Indians. Besides these there are in the United States very many other secret societies having for their end mutual beneficence, as Knights of Malta, Senate of Sparta, Knights of the Mystic Chain, Legion of the Red Cross, Knights of Friendship, Royal Arcanum. The Grand Army of the Republic was founded soon after the close of the civil war. Its members are veteran soldiers of that war. Its ends are to perpetuate the associations of comrades in arms, to relieve distress of members and provide benefit funds, and to advance the interests of the members in every honorable and lawful way. The badge of membership is a small bronze button worn in the coat lapel.

THE END

Index

About Am Rhyn

VAMzzz Publishing

Post **S**criptum

A comprehensive cultural history

Otto Henne am Rhyn

Otto Henne am Rhyn was born on August 26, 1828 in Sankt Gallen, Switzerland. He died on May 1, 1914 in Weiz, Styria, Austria-Hungary. He was a son of the historian Josef Anton Henne, called "von Sargans". After marrying Elisabeth am Rhyn, a member of the important Lucerne family Am Rhyn, he added her name to his own family name. Otto worked as a journalist and historian, and his comprehensive cultural history was a major contribution to the development of the German Kulturgeschichte (History of Civilization) school.

After studying at the Swiss universities of Bern and Geneva, he taught German, geography, and history at the local school at Sankt Gallen (1857–59). Later he served as an administrator of his canton and as its archivist. In 1861 he was admitted to the Concordia Lodge in St. Gallen, and from 1873 to 1878 he conducted the *Freimaurerzeitung* (Freemason News) in Leipzig, and joined the Loge Balduin in Leipzig.

Masonic literature owes him a great number of most valuable writings. These include Freemason rituals, rights and the supplementary volume of the second edition of the *Freemasonry Manual* (1879). In 1879 he returned to Switzerland to become the editor of the *Neue Zürcher Zeitung*. His greatest work is considered to be *Allgemeine Kulturgeschichte*, 8 vol. (1877–1908; *Universal History of Civilization*), from earliest times to the closing years of the 19th century. His other major book is *Kulturgeschichte des deutschen Volkes*, 2 vol. (1903; *Cultural History of the German People*). He also wrote cultural histories of the Swiss people, of Judaism, of the Crusades, and about the role of women in history. His publications were a forceful challenge to the traditional emphasis on political and military topics in German historiography.

The Nazis banned some of his books like a work entitled: *Prostitution und Mädchenhandel: Neue Enthüllungen aus d. Sklavenleben weißer Frauen u. Mädchen*, published after his death in Leipzig, 1922. They also banned Clarissa: *Aus dunklen Häusern Belgiens; Nach d. Franz Orig. von Alexis Splingard*, published in 1928, for which he wrote the introduction. These latter books reveal a criminal network dealing in sex slaves and underaged girls in Holland, Belgium and France.

'Masonic literature owes Otto Henne am Rhyn a great number of most valuable writings.'

Bibliography

- *Geschichte des Schweizervolkes und seiner Kultur. 3 Bände,* Leipzig.
- *Band 1,* 1865
- *Band 2,* 1865
- *Band 3,* 1866
- *Orts-Lexikon der Kantone St. Gallen und Appenzell.* St. Gallen 1868
- *Die Kulturgeschichte im Lichte des Fortschritts.* Leipzig 1869
- *Das Buch der Mysterien: Leben und Treiben der geheimen Gesellschaften aller Zeiten und Völker.* Leipzig 1869, 3. Aufl. 1891
- *Die deutsche Volkssage im Verhältniss zu den Mythen aller Zeiten und Völker.* Leipzig 1874
- *Allgemeine Kulturgeschichte von der Urzeit bis auf die Gegenwart, 8 Bände,* Leipzig.
- *Band 1: Die Urzeit und die morgenländischen Völker bis zum Verluste ihrer Selbständigkeit.* 1877
- *Band 2: Die Hellenen und Römer und ihr Machtgebiet.* 1877
- *Band 3: Das Mittelalter.* 1877
- *Band 4: Das Zeitalter der Reformation.* 1878
- *Band 5: Das Zeitalter der Aufklärung.* 1878
- *Band 6: Die neueste Zeit.* 1879
- *Band 7: Die jüngste Zeit.* 1897
- *Band 8: Die Kultur im Übergange vom 19. zum 20. Jahrhundert.* 1908
- *Kulturgeschichte des Judentums.* Jena 1880
- *Das Jenseits.* Leipzig 1881.
- *Kulturgeschichte des Deutschen Volkes. 2 Bände,* Berlin 1886

- *Kulturgeschichtliche Skizzen. 2. Aufl.*, Berlin 1889
- *Die Kultur der Vergangenheit: Gegenwart und Zukunft in vergleichender Darstellung.* 2 Bände, Leipzig 1890.
- *Die Freimaurerei in zehn Fragen und Antworten.* St. Gallen 1890 MDZ München
- *Die nationale Einigung der Deutschen, die Entwickelung und die Aufgaben des Reiches.* Hannover, 1891 Internet Archive
- *Der Teufels- und Hexenglaube: Seine Entwickelung, seine Herrschaft und sein Sturz,* Leipzig 1892
- *Kulturgeschichte des Jüdischen Volkes. 2. Aufl.,* Jena 1892
- *Eine Reise durch das Reich des Aberglaubens.* Leipzig 1893
- *Geschichte des Rittertums.* Leipzig 1894
- *Die Jesuiten, deren Geschichte, Verfassung, Moral, Politik, Religion und Wissenschaft.* 3. Aufl., Leipzig 1894
- *Geschichte des Kantons St. Gallen seit Annahme der Verfassung von 1861 bis auf die Gegenwart.* St. Gallen 1896
- *Anti-Zarathustra: Gedanken über Friedrich Nietzsches Hauptwerke.* Altenburg 1899.
- *Handbuch der Kulturgeschichte.* Leipzig 1900

'The Nazis banned some of his books.'

■

5

Paper books

VAMzzz Publishing

VAMzzz Publishing is located in the very centre of old Amsterdam, in The Netherlands. Our publishing company creates high quality revised editions of five star occult, witchcraft, Gothic and esoteric classics, mostly written in the Fin de siècle-period and early 20th century.

As a publisher, we deeply respect the writer of any book we choose, so we join our forces (top level graphic design & thirty years of occult studies) to produce enchanting volumes which maximize the reading pleasure and inform, often with extra added information. In contrast to the current trend of digital screen addiction, we think, this variety of literature needs to be presented on paper. *No e-books, but real books!*

Apart from re-publications of valuable but forgotten books, we are also in the preparation of new publications on topics such as self-healing, magic, new astrology and more.

VAMzzz Publishing
P.O. Box 3340
1001 AC Amsterdam
The Netherlands
contactvamzzz@gmail.com
www.vamzzz.com

Previews of all books including a complete table of contents can be viewed on www.vamzzz.com. More books will be added to the list. Please visit our website regularly for the latest updates.

Recommended

PAN Magazine
by VAMzzz Publishing
Free Online
www.vamzzz.com/pan.html

In Greek religion and mythology, PAN, the companion of the nymphs, is the god of the wild, shepherds and flocks, wild mountains and rustic music. He has the hindquarters, legs and horns of a goat, in the same manner as a faun or satyr. He is also recognized as the god of fields, groves and wooded glens; connected to fertility, the joy of life itself and the season of spring.

Though a mortal god in antiquity and an underground witch-god in medieval times, the last decades PAN has become a patron of both modern occultism, Wicca, paganism and the green guerilla – enthroned again as the one and only God of the Earth and Nature. PAN is the vibe touching those who refuse to become part of a machine, and who remain loyal to Mother Nature, the visible and hidden one. Therefore PAN is the most suitable icon we could chose for this periodical.

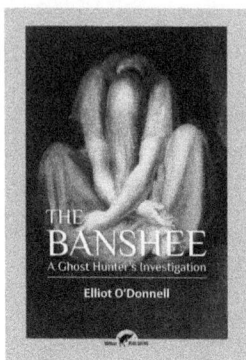

The Banshee
A Ghost Hunter's Investigation
by Elliot O'Donnell
222 pages, Paperback, ISBN 9789492355232

The banshee is a mysterious female spirit in Irish folklore, who heralds the death of a family member, usually by shrieking or keening. The screeching sound is described as somewhere between the wail of a woman and the moan of an owl, a low singing or piercing loud and able to break glass. The banshee appears as an old hag or beautiful lady, but may also appear as a crow, stoat, hare and weasel - animals associated in Ireland with witchcraft.

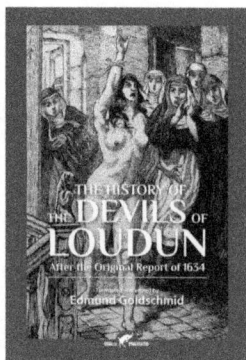

The History of the Devils of Loudun
After the Original Report of 1634
Translation by Edmund Goldschmid
118 pages, Paperback, ISBN 9789492355256

Around 1632 seventeen Ursuline Nuns were taken over by demons and went into a sexual and blasphemous state of hysteria for years. The work also describes the trial of a womanizing local priest named Father Urbain Grandier, who was accused of summoning these demons and, in the end, burned at the stake.

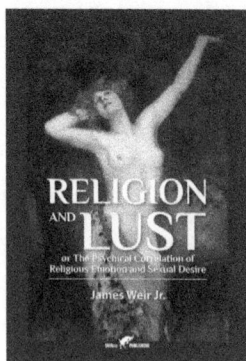

Religion and Lust
or The Physical Correlation of Religious Emotion and Sexual Desire
by James Weir Jr.
146 pages, Paperback, ISBN 9789492355270

In *Religion and Lust,* author James Weir Jr. investigates the origins of religious feeling, the once world wide spread fertility worship and the physical correlation of religious emotion and sexual desire. A major part of the work is filled with a colourful collection of religious or semi-religious, sexual rites, once practiced all over the globe, connecting the most "primitive" tribe to the most "civilized" nations.

Incubi and Succubi or Demoniality
A Historical Study of Sexual Contacts with Demons
by Sinistrari of Ameno
194 pages, Paperback, ISBN 9789492355263

This book is a revised English edition of Sinistrari's fascinating 17th century study on the orgasm-stimulating sex demon. The incubus and succubus are the same creature. The incubus is its male shape, copulates with women. The succubus visits men, triggering wet dreams. The intercourse with this astral visitor was called demoniality, a term no longer in use, though nowadays people are still having these mysterious incubus/succubus-"sexperiences".

Mysteria
History of the Secret Doctrines & Mystic Rites of Ancient Religions & Medieval and Modern Secret Orders
by Dr. Otto Henne am Rhyn
288 pages, Paperback, ISBN 9789492355225

Mysteria is a treasure box of missing conspiracy links and one of the very few publications, which offer reliable information about Adam Weishaupt's Illuminati for "the web & media-disinformed". Lodge-insider Otto Henne am Rhyn takes you on a journey, back to the Mystery cults of ancient Egypt, Babylon and Greece, passes Templars and explains modern lodges.

Magic and Magical Fetish
by Alfred Cort Haddon
108 pages, Paperback, ISBN 9789492355300

Alfred C. Haddon gives a practical and theoretical insight of the universal principles of magic, categorized in different techniques. The book is one of the very few works ever published, which describes wind and rain making. Magic is divided into sympathetic magic, the magic of words, talismans and divination, magical training routines. A kaleidoscope of forgotten magical techniques, which wasn't available for decades.

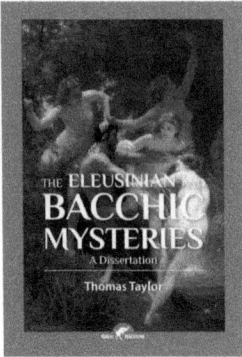

The Eleusian and Bacchic Mysteries
A Dissertation
by Thomas Taylor
200 pages, Paperback, ISBN 9789492355294

The Eleusian and Bacchic Mysteries focus on life, death and rebirth in a living nature (the present), while this nature was regarded as the converging of past and future. Taylor describes a series of lost secret rites. These rites were once the appointed means for regeneration through an inner union with the Divine Essence, despite their wild and sexual aspect.

Numbers
Their Occult Power and Mystic Virtues
by W. Wynn Westcott
170 pages, Paperback, ISBN 9789492355287

This book may be regarded as the "bible of numerology". It deals with Pythagorean number divisions, explains 3 different kinds of Kabalistic numerology, and reveals the hidden logic and symbolism of the numbers 1,2,3,4,5,6,7,8,9,10,11,12 and 13. This is accompanied by a long course of numbers between 14 and 25920. Special symbolisms are included like the link between numbers and planets and numbers in relation to the Apocalypse.

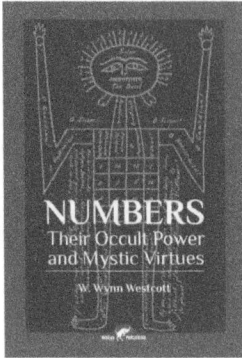

Sorceress
A Study of Witches and their Relations with Demons
by Jules Michelet
432 pages, Paperback, ISBN 9789492355249

This work is one of the most vivid, dark and confronting studies on witchcraft ever produced. Long before Murray's Witch-Cult in Western Europe, Michelet positions the medieval witch within a diminishing ancient culture of nature worship and the ruthless efforts of Christianity, with its cruel hostility towards nature, life (and women), to overwrite it. A nightmare of the most extraordinary verisimilitude and poetical power...

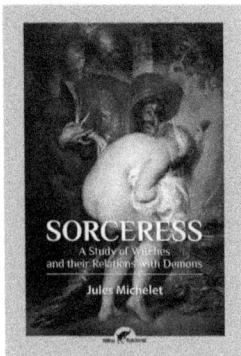

Aradia
Gospel of the Witches
by Charles Godfrey Leland
174 pages, Paperback, ISBN 9789492355010

This wonderful book describes the creation according to
Italian witch-lore. We also read about the witch-meeting
or sabbath (treguenda) and the book contains many
original magical recipes, like spells for love and good
fortune. Diana is further connected to the Moon and
the fairy world.

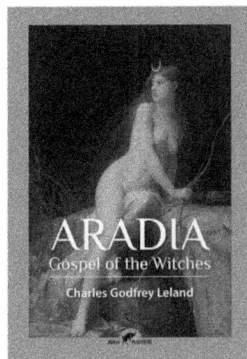

Demonology and Devil-Lore (Volume 1)
by Moncure Daniel Conway
490 pages, Paperback, ISBN 9789492355157

Demonology and Devil-Lore (Volume 2)
by Moncure Daniel Conway
518 pages, Paperback, ISBN 9789492355164

Within the demonology scope, this rare and mostly
forgotten, almost 1000 pages thick masterpiece, remains
unsurpassed in quality and completeness. Even in the
21st century the works offer fascinating missing links
for both the academic and student of occult traditions.
Moncure Daniel Conway divides Volume 1 in three
parts and deals mainly with the evolution and thematic
classification of ex-gods, demons and nature creatures.
Volume 2 deals primarily with the diabolic and with the
Devil himself, his ethnic history and connected topics.

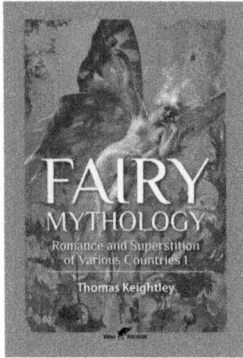

Fairy Mythology *(Volume 1)*
Romance and Superstition of Various Countries 1
by Thomas Keightley
404 pages, Paperback, ISBN 9789492355096

Fairy Mythology *(Volume 2)*
Romance and Superstition of Various Countries 2
by Thomas Keightley
404 pages, Paperback, ISBN 9789492355102

The term Fairy covers all kinds of nature spirits, not
just the tiny sugarsweet creatures hovering around
flowers. A unique and impressive book on this subject,
published in a revised 2 volume-edition. No wiccan
or pagan can afford to leave these books unopened.
About Elves, Dwarfs, Kobolds, Trolls, Changelings,
Meremaids, Nisses, Fairies, Brownies, Puck and other
Elemental spirits all over the world.

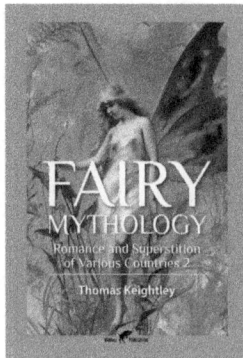

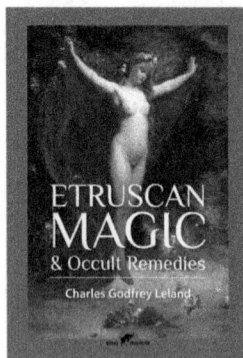

Etruscan Magic & Occult Remedies
(Two volumes in one book)
by Charles Godfrey Leland
628 pages, Paperback, ISBN 9789492355003

Part One of the book gives us a complete and detailed
insight in the Etruscan and Roman rooted pantheon of
the Tuscan Streghe (witches). Part Two describes many
of their spells, incantations, sorcery and several lost
divination methods. Much information in this book,
Leland received first hand from the Tuscan witches
Maddalena and Marietta.

Voodoos and Obeahs
Phases of West India Witchcraft
by Joseph J. Williams
374 pages, Paperback, ISBN 9789492355119

This work goes into great depth concerning the New World-African connection and is highly recommended if you want a deep understanding of the dramatic historical background of Haitian and Jamaican magic and witchcraft, and the profound influence of imperialism, slavery and racism on its development. Williams includes numerous quotations from rare documents and books on the topic.

Devil-worship in France
Or The Question of Lucifer
by Arthur Edward Waite
240 pages, Paperback, ISBN 9789492355065

In *Devil-Worship in France,* Waite attempts to discern what is genuine from what is fake in the evidence of 19th century Satanism. To get the answers he spends a great deal of time investigating the French Masonic echelon, debunking a "conspiracy of falsehood" and determining what should be understood by Satanism and what not. Huysmans' diabolical novel *Là-Bas* (1891) inspired Waite to write this sceptical analysis.

Testament of Solomon
A First Century AD Grimoire
76 pages, Paperback, ISBN 9789492355041

A first century AD grimoire, and therefore the oldest, and least known, of all grimoires (magical instruction books) in the occult tradition. The book describes health inflicting demons of zodiacal decans, summoned by King Solomon, and how he controlled them to use their forces to build his temple and more. Translated by F. C. Conybeare, appeared first in the *Jewish Quarterly Review* of October, 1898.

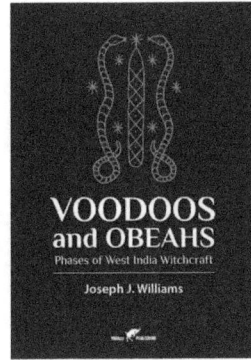

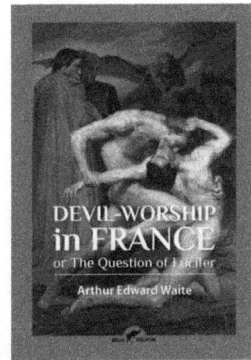

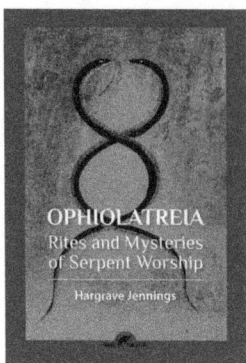

Ophiolatreia
Rites and Mysteries of Serpent Worship
by Hargrave Jennings
186 pages, Paperback, ISBN 9789492355126

An account of the rites and mysteries connected with the origin, rise and development of serpent worship in various parts of the world, enriched with interesting traditions, and a full description of the celebrated serpent mounds & temples, the whole forming an exposition of one of the phases of phallic, or sex worship.

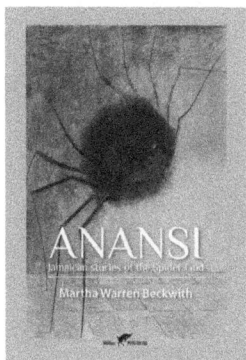

Anansi
Jamaican stories of the Spider God
by Martha Warren Beckwith
494 pages, Paperback, ISBN 9789492355171

Anansi is both a god, spirit and African folktale character. He often takes the shape of a spider and is considered to be the spirit of all knowledge of stories. He is also one of the most important characters of West African and Caribbean folklore.

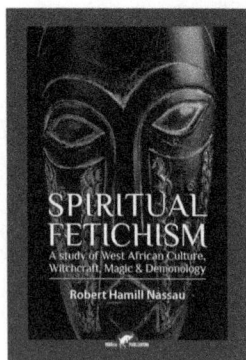

Spiritual Fetichism
A Study of West African Culture, Witchcraft, Magic & Demonology
by Robert Hamill Nassau
524 pages, Paperback, ISBN 9789492355188

Despite a nowadays anachronist and disturbing perspective, the book has remained most valuable for students of the occult, especially those interested in demonology, voodoo, hoodoo and its roots, African magick and religion, witchcraft, the classes of African spirits, and of course the spiritual and magickal use of a fetish.

Là-Bas
A Journey into the Self
by Joris-Karl Huysmans
378 pages, Paperback, ISBN 9789492355058

The plot of *Là-Bas* concerns the novelist Durtal, who is disgusted by the emptiness and vulgarity of the modern world. He seeks relief by turning to the study of the Middle Ages. Through his contacts in Paris, Durtal discovers that Satanism is not a thing of the past but alive and kicking in turn of the century France. The novel culminates with a description of a black mass.

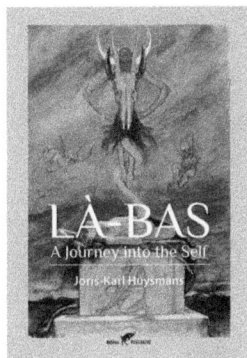

Unicorn
A mythological investigation
by Robert Brown Jr.
124 pages, Paperback, ISBN 9789492355072

Brown Jr. believes the unicorn to be a lunar symbol, and draws on mythology from a wide range of sources all over the world to build his case. The author discusses the heraldic use of the unicorn, relates the creature to ancient goddesses like Astarte, Hecate en the Gorgon Medusa, and provides the reader with lost esoteric Moon-lore.

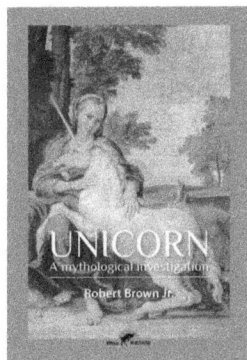

The House of Souls
A Fragment of Life / The White People
The Great God Pan / The Inmost Light
by Arthur Machen
336 pages, Paperback, ISBN 9789492355218

A collection of four masterpieces of horror and mystery, first collectively published in 1906. In the ingenious plot of *The Great God Pan,* a young woman is forced into Pan's reality, and turns into a femme fatale. *The Inmost Light* involves a doctor's scientific experiments into occultism and a vampiric force. In *The White People* a young girl's diary is discovered, describing her initiation into a secret world of folklore and ritual magic. In *A Fragment of Life* Machen tries to convince us of a hidden reality.

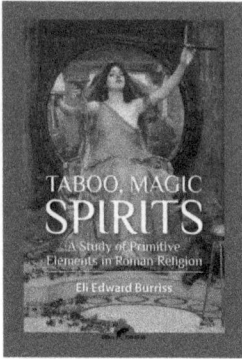

Taboo, Magic, Spirits
A study of primitive elements in Roman religion
by Eli Edward Burriss
200 pages, Paperback, ISBN 9789492355034

In Ancient Rome Mana was the term used for a mysterious, magical medium, which could be helpful or harmful (Taboo). Just like the Chinese qi, it could empower the positive and the negative. Contents: Mana, Magic and Animism – Positive and Negative Mana (Taboo) – Miscellaneous Taboos – Magic Acts: The General Principles – Removing Evils by - Magic Acts – Incantation and Prayer– Naturalism and Animism.

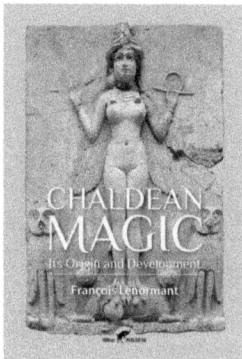

Chaldean Magic
It's Origin and Development
by François Lenormant
454 pages, Paperback, ISBN 9789492355027

The essentials of magic in Chaldea are presented inside a context of comparison or contrast to Egyptian, Median, Turanian, Finno-Tartarian and Akkadian magic, mythologies, religion and speech. Interesting is the Chaldean demonology, with its incubus, succubus, vampire, nightmare and many Elemental spirits, most of them coalesced with the primal powers of nature.

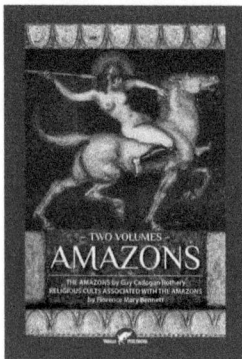

Amazons - *Two publications in one book -*
I. *The Amazons* by Guy Cadogan Rothery
II. *Religious Cults Associated With the Amazons*
    by Florence Mary Bennett
328 pages, Paperback, ISBN 9789492355089

Contents I: The Amazons of Antiquity – Amazons in Far Asia – Modern Amazons of the Caucasus – Amazons of Europe – Amazons of Africa – Amazons of America – The Amazon Stones. Contents II: The Amazons in Greek legend – The Great Mother – Ephesian Artemis – Artemis Astrateia and Apollo Amazonius – Ares.